D1568913

With Love
From Pet Heaven

Tum Tum, the Springer Spaniel

Dynasty
Press

Dynasty Press Ltd
36 Ravensdon Street
London SE11 4AR

www.dynastypress.co.uk

First published in this version by Dynasty Press Ltd, 2011.
ISBN: 9780955350795

Cover Artwork by James Empringham

Photography by David Chambers

Typeset by Strange Attractor Press

Printed and Bound in the United Kingdom

Acknowledgments

This book would not have been possible without the assistance of the many people who have generously given their time and energy. I would like to thank Gigi Michaels, my editor, for transcribing my thoughts and putting them onto paper; R.J. Day of Dynasty Press, who nursed this project from its inception to its realization; James Empringham for designing such a beautiful cover; Strange Attractor Press; David Chambers for using his photographic skills to enhance family snapshots and John Rendall for not only providing such a gracious comment about this book but for also being such a good and loving Pa to my daughter Bella.

I would also like to acknowledge the artistry of the late Caroline Leeds, whose sketch of me has been used for the cover.

Chapter One

As a Springer Spaniel, I find it amazing that so many supposedly intelligent human beings believe that Pet Heaven doesn't exist.

I remember an incident that illustrates the point perfectly. It took place while I was still earth-bound. My (human) mother was sitting beside me on the sofa in our sitting room in London, stroking the back of my neck as she often did, when one of her friends brought up the subject of Alan Clark, a well-known Member of Parliament who had recently died. "Of course, he was always frivolous," this friend said. "No MP should have behaved the way he did. But what convinces me that he was a complete idiot is what I heard over dinner last night. Can you believe he refused to convert to Catholicism because Father Michael Seed would not concede that he and his dogs would one day meet up in the After-Life? I ask you! What intelligent man, on his death-bed and wanting to convert to a church he regards as the one true faith, refuses to make the leap just because the priest who is instructing him in these matters decrees that dogs have no soul and therefore cannot join their masters in Heaven when they die?"

Well, you should have seen Ma's face. It was a veritable study in outrage. Even if I hadn't known her as well as I did after fourteen years of what she called Mother-and-Baby Love, I would have known that the condescending git who thought that it was Alan Clark who was a complete idiot, had strayed into rough terrain. For, before her features had set the way they did, I could scent trouble ahead. Literally smell it.

Of course, we Springer Spaniels have noses that are ten thousand times more efficient than the human version. We can pick up all sorts of odours that elude the most well-educated and informed people. This makes us way ahead of humans in our ability to accurately gauge the pros and cons of a situation as it unfolds. While the poor unfortunates who go through life on two feet have to use a lot of guess work, we simply sniff our way through the assortment of odours wafting up our nostrils the way shop attendants separate the jumbled pile of sale items shoppers discard in their quest for bargains.

"And, pray, why do you think Alan Clark was stupid for believing what many of us consider to be perfectly reasonable?" Ma said acerbically. "I think he was not only being sensible, but commendable.

You can hardly embrace a religion on your death-bed if you don't agree with its fundamentals. And what is more fundamental than the love people have for their pets? Or where we end up for all eternity?" It was apparent to both me and the humans present that Ma was struggling to abide by the maxim that a good hostess does not belittle her guests, even when they deserve it. But she wasn't being entirely successful in concealing her true feelings, for it wasn't

Typical evening en famillle with friends in London.

only her face that was a mask of underling irritation. Her tone of voice had enough edge in it to shave ice, and, to those of us who have acute nostrils, the sweet smell of the Nina Ricci *L'Air du Temps* which she used wasn't doing a very good job of masking the whiffs of annoyance that now intermingled with it.

I doubt that Ma's friend picked up the odour that her transgression had caused, but she certainly got the underlying message that Ma's tone of voice conveyed. I could detect that this friend was now retaliating with her own odours of annoyance, despite her best efforts to appear reasoned and calm. So when she shifted in her seat and said, in rather too patronising a way for my comfort or Ma's, "I know you love your pets, but you can't seriously think that they'll join you in Heaven one day?" you knew she was begging for trouble.

And trouble is what she got. My nostrils nearly exploded with an acrid odour akin to gunpowder, as Ma gritted her teeth and rasped from between them, with only the merest patina of politeness to mask what was quickly building up into real anger, "I don't know as a definite fact one way or the other, whether pets do go to heaven when they die. But nor do you - or anyone else for that matter. Since neither you nor I, nor anyone else in recorded history, has come back from the grave to tell us, I would suggest you refrain from belittling other people's beliefs and move onto a rather less contentious subject."

Terri, Ma's sometime assistant whom my human brother's Nanny had nicknamed Shadow because she was always around, was quick to step into the breech. Ever since her arrival on the scene a few years ago, she had set about eking out a position of indispensability for herself by making herself agreeable to one and all, but none more so than Ma. She never missed an opportunity to pacify Ma or her friends, even when there was no conflict. She perpetually took Ma's side, even when there was no cause to. What used to make me chuckle knowingly was the way she was always working herself into every conversation by asking questions to which she knew the answers. "Is that the same Father Michael Seed who was at your New Year's Eve party?" she now asked Ma, despite knowing very well that there was only one Father Michael Seed: The Pope's ecumenical advisor, and the priest famous for trying to convert any rich, famous or royal personage to Catholicism. His biggest fish would turn out to be Tony Blair when he stepped down as Prime Minister, but at that time he was still the head of government and intent on staying on as such, hence his self-serving profession of faith as an Anglican, despite the fact that Father Michael Seed came and went from Downing Street more regularly than the milkman, serving Mass and giving Communion to the most powerful Catholic-in-waiting in the western world in defiance of the Church's rule that only Catholics can take the Host.

"One and the same," Ma said, shots of sincerity wafting from her towards Shadow.

Ah Ma, poor Ma, I thought, what a pity it is that you can't smell that Shadow never gives off reciprocal fragrances. In fact, if you could bottle what emanates from her, you would have to label it self-interest.

"Isn't he the priest who converted the Duchess of Kent and Ann Widdicombe (another Tory Member of Parliament like Alan Clark)?" Shadow continued, the cloying scent of delight, which she always gave off when speaking about the Great and the Good, intermingling with the perpetual stench of self-interest. As any animal but homo sapiens knows, people who revere rank over feeling always sell others as well as themselves down the drain. The question isn't "If," but "When," "How" and "For what?"

I looked from Ma to her opinionated friend and to Shadow and back again. As I breathed in the atmosphere, it was clear to me that there were sub-texts to this human interchange that were far clearer to canines than the three humans involved. On one hand, Ma was only too cognizant of the solecism her friend had committed in stating that we doggies have no souls, but on the other, she was oblivious to the patent insincerity of Shadow's craven flattery and how she used self-abnegation to establish common ground with people she had nothing in common with. I could tell that Ma's friend, misguided though she was where Heaven was concerned, genuinely liked her, for she radiated affection through every pore.

As any dog can confirm, there are few more delightful fragrances under the sun than affection - and that includes food. But every time this friend, whose name I have forgotten, looked at Shadow, or listened to her, her pores closed up. It wasn't that she disliked her; so much as she was utterly indifferent. It was almost as if Shadow didn't exist where she was concerned. This wasn't the first time that I had detected this response to Shadow, and I often wondered if she could sense it. Not that I was unduly worried on her behalf, for ice rather than blood ran through her veins, and though she was consistently pleasant to everyone she ran across, whether she liked them or not, I could tell she didn't really care about anyone or most things, for the only time her pores were fragrant with pleasure was when the words "house in Chelsea", "lord", "duke" "royalty", "aristocracy", "party", "jewellery" and "furs" were mentioned. Then, and only then, would her body bestir itself to give off anything atavistic, and what an array of love and yearning would assault our poor nostrils.

But our olfactory glands are not the only gauge we doggies have to aid us with the truth. We also have a heightened sense of hearing. Everyone knows that we can hear sounds that no human being can. Our sense of pitch is so acute that you can use whistles to call us which you yourself cannot hear. But what might be less well known is that we use that ability as an additional adjunct to help us navigate our way through life with a degree of accuracy that would frighten you humans if you could only be aware of it. Your spouses, best friends, or children might be able to lie to you and get away with it. But they don't get away with deceiving us. We can pick up the merest shading of tone. This gives us a true reading of what you are really saying, and while you may be able to understand more words in the language you speak than we do (scientists say dogs can understand 200 words per language, though I can tell you that is a wild underestimation), we understand the underlying message of those words so much better than you that we are always ten steps ahead of any game you wish to play with each other.

"They say that no non-Catholic in public life is safe from Fr Seed's attentions," Ma's friend said, giving a wicked chuckle which was accompanied by the aroma of sincere delight. That alone would have told me that she was innocently mischievous.

Before Ma had a chance to open up her mouth and let out the

laugh that originated deep in her diaphragm, I could tell what her reaction would be. She loved a good laugh, especially if it was naughty. She was also a firm believer that God wasn't a snob. She was always decrying priests who pandered to the rich and powerful without endowing the less privileged with equal respect. She often said, "I honestly cannot believe that God prefers dukes to dustmen, or millionaires to machinists. I'm still shopping for a priest who sees me as a soul whose value has nothing to do with worldly advantage. Until then, I will just have to muddle my way through to a better understanding of what God intends for us on my own, without the guidance of a priest. "

It therefore came as no surprise to me when Ma roared with laughter, aroma-ing (my word to describe the delightful scents that are an inevitable result of genuine pleasure) and tinkling the room joyously at the wicked thought of Father Seed busily collecting eminent scalps for the Church of Rome.

As she was doing so, I looked from Ma to Shadow and back again. Shadow shifted in her chair. Any dog could tell what was coming before she formed the words. The flat odour of yearning, which is so characteristic of the emotionally vacant, provided an unwelcome antidote to the heady delights that both Popsie Miranda, my daughter who was sitting on Ma's other side, and I were enjoying while Ma and her other friend were enjoying a real laugh. "He never remembers me. I suppose that's because I'm not important enough for him to remember," Shadow said plaintively, a range of negative emotions choking her vocal chords so that they functioned an octave above where pleasure would have pitched them.

Oi, gevalt, I thought: Here we go again. Shadow always managed to work herself into the epicentre of every conversation, usually employing the tool of self-pity when agreeability wasn't appropriate.

"I'm sure that's not so," Ma said, more out of a desire to console than to disagree.

"It **is** true," Shadow insisted even more plaintively than before. "So few of your friends ever remember me. Take Liz for instance. I've met her maybe twenty times, and each time it's as if it's the first."

Popsie Miranda had been sitting quietly, her eyes closed while Ma stroked the base of her ear the way she loved it, but now she shifted her body.

"Liz is as blind as a bat and cannot wear contact lenses but refuses to wear glasses. The reason why she never recognizes you is that she most likely has never seen you," Ma said, intent on consoling Shadow while also patting Popsie Miranda on her back in an attempt to settle her.

Now, the one thing that Popsie Miranda had never been able to stand was conflict. The contrasting odours, vibrations and sounds which were so much a feature of human interchange, and which I actually enjoyed because I loved sorting through them in a quest for the truth, were now becoming too intense for my daughter. So she shook herself free from Ma's touch, raised her perfectly formed head and sat up with all the grace and elegance that were ingrained features of her personality. I confess my heart swelled with pride as yet again I had cause to remember the comment of Dr Simon Mayer, the Vet at Elizabeth Street, when he told Ma, "Popsie Miranda is the most beautiful bitch in dogdom. She is like the young Brigitte Bardot - the quintessence of feminine pulchritude."

Don't think that my pride was anything but humble appreciation. Although Popsie Miranda was my daughter, I was mindful of the fact that I was not really responsible for the manifest beauty she was. That was a genetic fluke beyond my control. And she was physically perfect. Her body, head and limbs struck everyone who saw her, whether man, woman, doggie or indeed crow, as ideally proportioned. She had the most exquisite face – perfect nose, marvellous forehead, wonderful ears, luscious mouth, and big, beautiful brown eyes with long black lashes. But what took her out of the realms of beauty into the pantheon of perfection was the way she moved. Popsie Miranda did not walk – she gracefully waggled and wiggled, like Marilyn Monroe on four legs. Her tail had been docked when she was five days old, and when she waggled the stub her bottom rotated in such a way that even the quintessential Blonde Bombshell could have learnt a thing or two about feminine appeal.

Nor did her splendour cease when she was in repose. Popsie

Miranda sitting down was an array of artistic poses, never contrived, always natural: one of her front legs bent graciously in a picture of elegance that was as innate as the colour of her fur. She truly was the living embodiment of grace and beauty at all times.

As I looked at this beautiful creature I had given birth to, it was obvious that the atmosphere in Ma's drawing room had become too charged for her. She shot me a look which said, "Enough is enough. I'm off." She gave Ma's hand a gentle little lick as a precursor to leave-taking, and slithered off the sofa, making her way upstairs to lie on the bed we shared with Ma.

"Good night Popsie," Shadow said unctuously, stretching out her hand to pat her as she walked past. Hypocrite, I thought, giving a little yelp, and remembered the time, three years beforehand, when we had had the misfortune to stay with her. Ma had gone on a cruise up the Nile with our three year old (human) brothers and their nurse. Normally, when Ma travelled, Nanny stayed at home with us. It wasn't ideal, for she never took us out for walks in the park the way Ma did, but at least she fed us properly, let us out into the garden regularly and frequently, so that we could do our business and sniff the air, and when she returned from her daily walk in the park with the Boys, as everyone called our human brothers, they would play with us. Nanny didn't pretend to like dogs, but she was conscientious in respecting Ma's regimen for us, and moreover encouraged the *boys* to play with us, with the result that we had the opportunity to give and receive the love we all needed, whether Ma was around or not.

I wish I could say the same for Shadow. She was always pretending to like us when Ma was around, doubtless because she knew this was a sure-fire way to obtain Ma's good opinion. She would greet us sweetly, make cooing noises, and drive home the point of what a wonderful person she was for Ma's benefit by invariably patting one of us as we ambled by her. But she was being insincere. We dogs could pick up that she didn't care about us at all. With our enhanced sensory perceptions, we could smell the disinterest and pick up the decibel level of well-masked insincerity to which all humans are deaf. More than once, we agreed between ourselves that it must a nightmare to be human and have to go through life with so limited an ability to pick up the plethora of scents and sounds which canines use to safely navigate our way through the complexities of life. Which is how Ma came to inflict us with the experience of staying with Shadow.

It was December 1996. Ma dropped us off at Shadow's, which was actually a beautiful four storey Queen Anne house on one of London's large squares. Walks should therefore have been no problem. But exercise was anathema to Shadow, who, we discovered soon enough, spent her whole time sprawling on the sofa or lying in bed, frequently with her flaccid ex-banker boyfriend Kevin, whom she was eager to marry because he had a house in Chelsea while hers was in unfashionable Camden. Never once did she open the front door to take us across the street to the square, which had beautifully mown grass where doggies promenaded throughout the daylight hours with their proud owners. We were reduced to staring at the action across the street from her drawing room windows, where we would sit ticking off the hours until Ma returned to rescue us from this seemingly-homely but sterile prison.

At least, we would reflect gratefully as we saw the world go by from the drawing room, Shadow hadn't kept us locked out in her back yard the way she sometimes did. On those occasions, we really suffered. The boredom was excruciating. The back garden, as Shadow pretentiously called it, was a few feet of concrete surrounded by a high wooden fence, dustbins which were taken out for collection so seldom that Shadow had four where most households had one, and a 'garden' door which she never once opened for the duration of our visit. Popsie Miranda and I would be reduced to sitting around staring at each other with nothing to occupy us once we had done our business. Which leads me to another problem. Shadow was so intent on saving herself the effort entailed in opening the door to let us out into the garden four or five times a day, that she would leave us outside for hours on end.

This was bad enough when the weather was good, but December in London is not warm even when it is dry, and on more than one occasion we were made to sit in the freezing rain without any prospect of shelter. Worse than that, however, was the time she left us outside all day in the midst of a thunder storm. There was so much lightning that Popsie Miranda and I had to ask ourselves if she thought she was training us for starring roles in a *son et lumiere* production. We agreed that it was just as well that Maisie Carlotta wasn't with us. This granddaughter of mine through Popsie Miranda was terrified of thunder and lightning and always sought refuge under Ma's bed whenever there was a storm. Fortunately for us all, she was on honeymoon with her husband Rupert Van Der Linden, at his parents' house in Chelsea. There, she was being treated like royalty by Henry and Cam Van Der Linden, who were desperate to have a son from Rupert, their American Springer Spaniel. They didn't even turn a hair when Maisie Carlotta and Rupert, locked in ecstasy for the second time that day, knocked over a table containing a precious vase as they twirled round and round the Sloane Avenue West drawing room in the canine version of an impassioned waltz.

The reaction of the Van Der Lindens to that accident perfectly illustrated the difference between them and Shadow. They gently moved Rupert and Maisie Carlotta away from the broken bits, in case they cut their paws, and once they separated naturally, Mr and Mrs Van Der Linden stroked and patted Maisie almost as much as they stroked Rupert.

Meanwhile, while Popsie Miranda and I were house-guesting with Shadow, she deemed it unnecessary to give either of us even one pat, on the grounds that, since Ma wasn't around to pass judgement on her performance, she could skip the pretence. Worse, she never fed us breakfast before mid-day; and often failed to abide by Ma's instructions that she also give us dinner at around eight o'clock in the evening, with the result that we often went to bed – I should say went to sleep on the floor - ravenous.

But the most humiliating thing was the infrequency with which she let us out of the house when she wasn't keeping us outside for half the day. Though she told Ma she would follow her regimen of letting us out into the garden every four or five hours for us to do our business, and faithfully promised to take us across the square every morning for a long walk, not only did she fail to take us for one walk for the nine days she had us, but she frequently ignored the fact that we couldn't open her 'garden' door ourselves. Sometimes, we were so desperate for relief that we would bark to remind her that we were in the house and needed to be let out. Incredibly, she would bark right back at us, snapping that we should shut up and she would let us out when she was ready.

The problem with Shadow was that she seldom felt like doing anything but lying in bed or on the sofa with or without that huge blob of an ex-banker called Kevin. On two separate occasions she delayed and delayed and delayed so long that first Popsie Miranda, then I, had accidents. You can imagine how mortified we were. Both Popsie and I were fastidiously clean and proud of how well-regulated we were. To be reduced by the laziness and inconsideration of one of Ma's supposed friends to making a puddle, as I did, or doing poohs, as Popsie Miranda did, was humiliating in the extreme.

After such callous treatment, we decided that we wanted to have nothing more to do with Shadow. Up to that point, we had been tolerant enough of her advances. But the time had come to stop being so accommodating. So thereafter we never wagged our tails at her ever again, not even when she laid our bowls of feed down for us in the remaining days of our visit.

Never were we happier to see Ma than when she came to pick us up from Shadow's house. We bolted straight to her and the *boys*, covering them with licks, kisses and yelps of delight as our tails went wild with joy as well as relief.

While they were responding with the human version of licks and kisses accompanied by a wealth of strokes and pats, Popsie Miranda and I shoved them in the direction of the front door. We could smell the Jaguar parked right outside the door.

"My goodness, you are eager to depart," Ma said laughingly. "If I didn't know better, I would think you hadn't enjoyed being Terri's houseguests."

"They were good as gold. A real pleasure to have around. I'll be happy to keep them again if you ever need me to," Shadow said.

Popsie Miranda and I promptly started to yap, trying to inform Ma how nightmarish the stay had been. The problem with human beings, however, is that they are really very limited linguistically. Not only do they not speak any other species' language, but even the most erudite of linguistics can manage only a handful of human languages. And they certainly don't have a universal tongue the way we animals do. Doggie is doggie irrespective of whether we are a Doberman from Darmstadt or a Rhodesian Ridgeback from Rio de Janeiro. An English dog doesn't need anyone to translate the bark of a French dog, though, like humans, we will need translation if you speak to us in a human tongue we have not learnt. For instance, telling me to sit in Spanish would have evoked the same response as asking any non-Spanish-speaking human to understand the same command. But I used to watch the television and could understand everything a Spanish dog communicated, as long as it was in canine talk.

Why humans persist in calling us 'dumb' animals when we all speak a language we can understand, but which they cannot, is beyond me. Did you know that animal linguistics are so universal that monkeys in the jungle screech a warning when leopards are stalking prey that other monkeys and indeed even crows understand?

I am sure you can guess what is coming. Ma, the *boys*, Nanny and I all piled into the car, everyone yapping in their own tongue, with Popsie Miranda and me at total cross purposes with Ma, who kept on responding to our information about how Shadow had treated us with such inappropriate but nevertheless loving comments as, "Yes, my darlings, I am happy to see you too." Once or twice she even yapped back at us, as was her wont when she wanted to 'relate to us on our own level', as she would put it in human-speak. Of course, we found her attempts endearing, but what she didn't know was that her sounds made no sense at all, for humans haven't yet evolved to the stage where they can emulate doggie yaps, yelps and barks and convert the sounds into intelligible dog-talk.

If humans like Father Seed had any doubt about whether we dogs have souls, they should have witnessed the way we dealt with Shadow after that visit. Every time she saw us and bent down to pat our heads and said, in that saccharine tone of voice she employed to make the adults listening think how sweet she was, "Hello Tum Tum. Hello Popsie Miranda. How are you girls? Have you missed your Aunt Terri?" I would graciously receive the pat without responding in my normally affectionate manner; neither wagging my tail nor licking her, but Popsie Miranda was the real card. She would snort derisively and pointedly walk off, as if to say, "You brazen hypocrite. Why don't you take your phoney friendliness elsewhere?" It didn't take long for Ma to notice, either, for she took to saying to Shadow, "Popsie Miranda seems to have developed a tremendous sense of hauteur with age. " But even Ma, responsive as she was to us, didn't add up two and two and come up with the fact that we were pointedly snubbing Shadow, and had been doing so ever since she had been inflicted upon us as our hostess, for the simple reason that we did not like her.

It was disappointing to us that Ma never made the leap from our aloofness to the reason why we felt as we did. But then, as Popsie and I had decided, we had to cut Ma some slack. She was, after all, only human. Although we had tried, time and again, to bark the message out to her, she didn't understand Doglish as comprehensively as we did English – a failing, I fear, shared by all other humans, no matter how well disposed they are towards doggies. She therefore missed our message, with consequences that would ultimately be regrettable for her even more than for us, for the day would come when Ma would see how insincere Shadow was, and when she did, she would be sorely disappointed.

Chapter Two

I was an authentic lovechild, conceived to be the living embodiment of my human parents' love.

Pa and Ma were having something that we canines find inconceivable: a real, passionate, enduring romance. Although everyone knows that there is no one more loving or loyal than a dog, hence why we have earned the reputation for being man's best friend, we simply do not function in such a restrictive way. Whom we love, we love passionately and devotedly. There is no link between our enduring passions and romance, which in my opinion Nature has sensibly linked to our seasons. Had it done so with homo sapiens as well, you can be sure the human world would have been as happy and peaceable as life is in the doggie world, where in the ordinary course of events important considerations like survival and sociability count for far more than romantic satisfaction.

One could almost say that the natural inclinations of dogs accord with those of human beings over the age of forty. Like mature adults, we are free from the biological connection between reproduction and love in our everyday life.

Like many younger people, however, we do find ourselves in the teeth of physical passion when we are in season, the difference being that our seasons are finite and twice a year, while theirs are constant for years on end. This is an important distinction between the ways our two species perform, for during our seasons we do throw over the equitable devotion which is otherwise such a feature of our species. In doing so, we function for those few weeks like your young people.

As we too surrender to the lure of reproductive passion, we become as intent on scoring as any young woman or man in one of those singles' bars or nightclubs that proliferate on both sides of the Atlantic. The results can be as chaotic as anything in the human world, with the exception that we usually resort to biting each other, while they usually couch their ferocity behind less frank but equally disagreeable conduct.

At times like those, the parallels between humans and canines prove that many humans are exactly like us when we are in season. They too keep their physical needs completely separate from love. While that has the merit of keeping some of the heat out of romantic competitiveness, it also has the unwanted consequence of increasing the opportunities for disappointment in those who want lasting relationships rather than transient physical gratification – a complication from which we doggies are fortunately spared by nature.

I have now had an opportunity to observe how humans perform both from an earthly and a heavenly perspective, and I have come to the conclusion that most people really want to be the way Ma and Pa were when I was born. They prefer love to accompany lust.

To me, human relationships are endlessly fascinating. I suppose I always had a natural predisposition in that direction, and this was fostered by my early – and happy -experiences. Ma and Pa truly loved each other; to such an extent that sometimes you would have thought they were dogs. They were very playful as well as affectionate, not only with each other and with me, but with other people and other dogs as well. They had similar senses of humour, and the only thing they seemed to like more than laughing was stroking and kissing.

They had met when they were both young: Ma twenty six, Pa twenty nine. Both had been married once before. While Pa's first marriage ended on a civilized note, the same cannot be said of Ma's. Against her will, her ex-husband dragged her thorough a bitter and protracted divorce which left her traumatized and deeply sceptical of further emotional involvement.

From the moment Pa met her in the fashionable London club Annabel's, he knew she was the woman for him. Although it took him a few months to get her to the point where she reciprocated, once she had surrendered herself, she was equally committed to their romance. Like many young lovers, they found it impossible to be apart for any length of time. And like many young and compatible lovers, they were never happier than when together.

Although they did not live together, they spent more time together than most married couples. They started each day with a run around Hyde Park, separating while Pa went to work as a stockbroker in the City of London and Ma went home to Belgravia to write. After work, they invariably met up and were frequently out together socially in the evenings. Sometimes, they even got together for lunch, which I used to enjoy, for Ma usually took me along for the ride.

They had been together for nine years when they decided to crown their romance with a lovechild. Babies were out of the question. Pa already had three children and did not want any more, and while Ma hankered after babies and would ultimately adopt two in the years to come, they decide to have a puppy instead.

Nor could it be any old puppy. This lovechild, who would live with Ma, had to be the progeny of Pa's beloved Springer Spaniel, Sootie, who lived with Pa and ran around Hyde Park with him and Ma each morning.

This plan might sound like a sorry substitute for a baby to people who do not love dogs, but Ma and Pa were passionate dog-lovers. As anyone who knows pet-lovers will appreciate, many people love their animals more than their friends and relations. Some even more than their children. Or, as Ma would often say in the years to come, "The only people I love more than my pets are my two children."

Pa was a very take-charge kind of guy who acted upon decisions. Once he and Ma had therefore agreed that Sootie would produce their lovechild, he immediately set the wheels in motion and arranged a suitable marriage for her with one of his nephew's star studs. Naturally, this sire was another Springer Spaniel, as beautiful and healthy and good-natured as Sootie.

Pa and Ma now sat back and waited for Sootie to come into season. The optimum time for a productive union is not at the beginning of the season, but after the second week. As Pa did not want to be without his Sootkins, as he called my canine mother, for one day longer than he had to be, he did not take her up to his ancestral home in the Borders of Scotland until she was well into the second week of her season.

To ensure that conception took place, he left Sootie with her husband for a whole week. It's just as well he did so, for I was not conceived until the 2nd June 1985, and had he not taken that precaution, Sootie would have had a lot of fun but Ma and Pa would not have had the lovechild they wanted.

As it was, the initial ceremony took place in the kennels, with Pa and the gamekeeper as witnesses, after which Pa retired to the main house for the weekend, leaving Sootie to enjoy the attentions of her new husband in their own stall.

However, this was a far from ideal arrangement. There was a quantity of other dogs, mostly Springer Spaniels or hounds, in the kennels, and though they did not have access to Sootie, they certainly had access to the delicious pheromones her season was spraying throughout the atmosphere. They too wanted to join in on the honeymoon, and they were not bashful about announcing their desire. As the kennels degenerated into a cacophony of barks of ever-increasing volume and intensity, the noise became so overwhelming that the gamekeeper finally took pity on all the other dogs, who were being frustrated by not being a part of the honeymoon, and transferred the newly-weds to his own cottage.

Dogs cannot get pregnant towards the end of their seasons. Once ovulation has passed, the sex act becomes extraneous to the reproductive process, and the female of the species ceases to enjoy the carnal attention she has until then relished from the male. She begins to spurn his attentions, which of course frustrates him, for the pungent pheromones that still emanate from her continue to compel him to

17

persist in the activities they have been so recently enjoying.

Knowing this, Pa resolved to have Sootie back with him in London at the earliest opportunity, so within a week he was back in Scotland to drive her down to London. The way Pa fell upon Sootie, with hugs and kisses and nuzzles and grunts, would have convinced even the stony-hearted that greater love hath no man than for his dog.

Sootie, it has to be said, also made it clear where her priorities lay. Honeymoons were one thing, but Pappy and Baby Love were another matter altogether. As she lived up to the springer aspect of our breed by jumping onto Pa's lap and leaving paw prints on his freshly-laundered green corduroy trousers, the stub of her tail wagging at such a rate it looked as if it might fall off, you could tell that she couldn't wait to get back to the creature comforts of their London house, where she and he often watched television curled up together on the sofa.

Neither Pa nor Ma could tell for the first few weeks if Sootie was pregnant, but once her pregnancy became obvious, they were so excited you would have thought they were having me themselves. As she grew larger by the day, they bathed her in ever-increasing doses of affection and congratulation. From the inside looking out, it was very reassuring to know that I would be going to such a loving home – the only problem being that I might not be the one chosen, for there were six of us, and in the womb it was impossible to know who was a boy and who was a girl. And Pa and Ma wanted only a girl.

Sootie's due date fell within the week of the 5th August 1985. Because no one knew exactly when conception had taken place, they could be no more precise than that. 'Whelping' was a common occurrence at Pa's ancestral home in Scotland, so he decided to take Sootie back there for her confinement. He therefore drove her up yet again, left her there along with his Mercedes estate car for when he came to collect her and the puppies, and flew back to London from Edinburgh.

If Pa thought that Sootie was going to be kept in the house, he was wrong. No sooner had he left for the airport than she was taken over to the kennels, where she stayed for the remainder of her pregnancy.

Sootie was not best pleased, I can tell you. She was used to the creature comforts of a London house. Scotland in August can be awfully chilly, and she definitely missed the warmth of her Kensington residence. What she did not miss, however, was the cleanliness. The multiplicity of scents emanating from the straw bedding in the kennels were just one of the delights you can't get in city properties. Also, instead of the splendid isolation of London, where she was the only pet in the house, she had what seemed like an endless supply of companions in Scotland, for the estate had a shoot. This translated into a variety of gundogs who came into their own during the shooting season, which more or less coincided with her arrival there, the Glorious 12th (of August) being the day the British shooting season starts officially.

The gamekeeper was a dog-lover, and he used to talk to and pat Sootie along with the various other dogs, all of whom were gun-dogs. Only too quickly, Sootie, who was so used to loving and being loved by Pa that she attracted affection wherever she went, had managed to inveigle her way into a special place in his heart, and thereafter he singled her out for special attention.

As Sootie arrived the week before the Glorious 12th, her timing in terms of enjoyable activities could not have been more perfect. All the gundogs were exercised every day, preparatory to fulfilling their function of retrieving the game as it was downed. Though she was heavy with children, Sootie still loved exercise as much as any other spaniel. Though she had to take things a bit easy and slow down the bounding she customarily did, she nevertheless was thrilled to be in the country, breathing the fresh air, taking in the many scents and sounds, sniffing paths and routes with her many companions, and generally availing herself of the wealth of pleasures open to country dogs living the optimum country life.

Humans might not be aware of it, but dogs are every bit as conscious of their ancestry as their masters. I was and remain as proud of my heritage as any descendant-worshipping citizen of China can be. I have become even more aware since crossing over from my earthly existence to Heaven how important it is to appreciate the gifts and merits with which one was blessed at birth. And I had a lot to be grateful for. Both my canine parents came from a long line of gun-dogs.

Springer Spaniels are one of the oldest pure breeds in existence. We were at the Courts of King Henry VII and VIII in the fifteenth and sixteenth centuries. We even sailed on the Mayflower to America with the brethren who landed at Plymouth Rock. We are excellent at retrieving game. We have a sense of smell that is superior to most other dogs. We are also loving by nature as well as intelligent, with the result that we are easy to train. We are loyal and obliging which makes us ideal pets as well as retrievers. Our mouths are soft and that, allied to our gentle nature, means that we always bring back the game that the guns fell without damaging or worse, devouring, it.

Those of you who travel will also be aware that in recent times our traditional role as retrievers has been expanded. Any passenger touching down at one of the main airports will see our breed sniffing arriving passengers and their luggage in the Customs halls of American and European airports, as the Customs officials who are our handlers follow in the wake of our wagging tails.

On many an occasion, a passenger will remark on how obvious it is that we enjoy our work, for we go from person to person, sniffing enthusiastically as our tails wag rhythmically from side to side. Yes, it is true. We do enjoy hunting and retrieving, which is of course what we are doing as we sniff passengers in our search for drugs and other contraband. And we do so not only with enthusiasm but also with finesse, for we are one of doggiedoms most gentle and energetic breeds.

Being medium sized, we also make ideal pets. Many people don't want the burden of a large dog like an Alsatian or a Labrador any more than they desire the lapdogs which are so fashionable amongst 'ladies who lunch'. We are therefore deemed to be the ideal compromise in terms of size and disposition.

On the other hand, we are also good guard dogs, because we have powerful lungs and a healthy bark, and we do not hesitate to use them when someone is invading our territory. Although not fierce by nature, we would not hesitate to fight off an attacker or invader, so I suppose our reputation for possessing an ideal combination of qualities, which make us superb pets as well as effective working dogs, is justified.

On the 5th August, 1985, Sootie's labour pains began. She duly prepared the bedding the way all bitches do when they are about to whelp. Having rearranged the straw to her satisfaction, she lay down and started to pant her way through the flurry of movement which was emanating from her insides. When the gamekeeper realized that she was about to give birth, he kept dropping in to see how she was progressing. Once or twice he even removed the cowls from the newborn puppies' bodies, though he was careful to leave the placenta for her to devour, as this not only protects the mother but also the puppy.

I was the third puppy to come into the world, immediately after a brother who looked exactly like me – same head, markings, even size – and before a liver and white sister. Not everyone knows that liver and white are the original colours of spaniels, with the result that most large litters of a black and white sire and dam will produce both black and white and liver and white puppies. Indeed, when my granddaughter Maisie Carlotta gave birth to nine puppies, three were tricolours – black, liver and white – four were black and white, and two were purely liver and white.

I, however, was black and white. That was just as well, for, had I not been, Ma would have chosen someone else, her heart having been set on having a black and white puppy.

For the first nine weeks of my life, I stayed in the kennels in Scotland. Those were happy, secure days. Sootie was a good mother: loving, attentive, and full of an inexhaustible supply of delicious milk. The other dogs in the kennels were not allowed into our stall, lest they infect us with strange diseases like the parvo virus, but even if they had been, Sootie would not have wanted them near us. She was very protective of her brood, and growled at anyone who approached us except for the gamekeeper and his daughter. That included our canine father, whose interest in his progeny was rewarded by a snarl when he tried to sniff around our bedding.

Life dishes out its jolts to all of us. Whether man or dog, not even halcyon days can last forever. My first jolt came when I was about six weeks old. I wriggled towards Sootie for some of that delectable ambrosia which I was in the habit of suckling from one of her many teats, when she suddenly snarled at me and pulled away. I quivered, quaked and whimpered until she relented and let me onto the breast. I did not know it then, but my baby teeth were coming out and this was nature's way of moving both mother and puppy on to the next stage of our development. And though Sootie did relent on this the first occasion, within days she was actually running away with such decisiveness from all of us when we wanted to be fed that we soon got the message that there would be no more liquid emanating from her lush teats.

The gamekeeper, well versed in the various stages of puppy development, now started to lay down bowls of puppy food for us, and within two weeks, all of us puppies had been weaned and Sootie once again let us snuggle up to her, this time purely for Mummy and Baby cuddles.

Although we did not know it, this stage signalled separation. We were now eight weeks old, the age when people customarily take possession of their puppies. But Pa had a theory that puppies must be given away at nine weeks, not eight. He had read somewhere that we do not experience fear until we are eight weeks old. "It is cruel to separate them from their litter just as they are becoming aware of fear. It makes them neurotic for the rest of their lives, and I want Sootie's puppies to be fearless, not nervous," he declared.

So he and Ma didn't come for us until we were nine weeks old. Although I did not remember the first time I saw Ma and Pa while I was on earth, since coming to Pet Heaven I am no longer limited by restrictions like memory and time, and having unfettered access to both the past and the future, I can see the afternoon of Sunday, 5th October, 1985 as clearly as you can see this sentence. It was drizzling – something it does an awful lot of in Scotland, as all of us who have a Scottish connection can attest to – and you could tell by the nip in the air that winter was fast approaching. I could hear the gamekeeper talking in the distance to a strange man and woman, whose voices became ever more distinct as they approached the stall where we were ensconced. Unlike dogs, who have no accents, this man and woman spoke in an entirely different way from the man who had been feeding us for the last few weeks. This alone made me sit up and pause.

Before I had time to make sense of this new fact, we were all confronted by this strange-sounding couple. They were so exuberant that we would have been flooded with a positive tsunami of emotion even if Sootie had not jumped up and started to yelp as they approached, springing left, right and centre in a maelstrom of joyousness. Although most of us whose tails have been docked would prefer to have retained the glorious flags of communicativeness with which nature endowed us, on this occasion we were all rather selfishly relieved that Sootie had had her tail docked, for it was rotating with such ferocity that she would have flayed us to within an inch of our lives if it had been its original length.

"Sootkins, how *are* you, my magnificent girl?" the man with the strange accent said in such a kindly tone that I knew then and there that he loved her as devotedly as Sootie loved him. She was now so demented with rapture that she was rotating wildly, leaping here, there, and everywhere while yapping out professions of love.

Like humans, dogs need time to learn any language. Of course, we are far quicker on the uptake, where communication between our own species is concerned, than humans. Sootie, however, had not so far had the opportunity to introduce us to her Pa, but as she yelped delightedly, I understood that she was telling him how overjoyed she was to see him, and how she hoped he would like the puppies she had had for him.

For his part, Pa possessed an uncanny knack of understanding exactly what Sootie was saying. "Yes, my beautiful Sootkins, I've missed you madly too. Shall we look at your puppies? Yes, you think that's a good idea? Well, come on, you effect the introductions," he said, laughing good-naturedly as he did so.

So far, the lady accompanying him had said nothing, though she did pat Sootie affectionately as our canine mother led the way into the stall to inspect her brood. As soon as this slender blonde saw us, however, she too became exultant. "Aren't they the cutest puppies? Sootie, you've done us proud," she said, love oozing out of every pore and inflection.

"Which one do you want?" Pa said.

"I don't really know? They're all so adorable I'm not sure I can choose."

"You can't have all six," Pa said, bending over to peck her on the cheek. With that, he stooped over the basket, picked each of us up individually, then, when he came to me, said, "What about this one? She's a real beauty, and she's black and white."

The strange lady, whom I would grow to know and love as Ma, held out her hand. She had long painted nails and a big shiny stone set in a white metal which I would subsequently learn was a diamond set in platinum. She cupped this left hand with her right, and Pa placed me in them.

"She is beautiful," she said, stroking me with her index finger. As Pa's attention diverted to the game-keeper and the other puppies, Ma started to talk to me. "Would you like to come and live with me? I'd consider myself very lucky indeed to have such a beautiful puppy as you. Do you know, I even have a name for you already? Would you like to know what it is? It's Tum Tum. A funny old name, I'm sure you'll think, but when your Pa first mooted the idea of having our own lovechild through Sootie, I was lying on his tummy and told him that I would name you in honour of it as a memento of a very precious moment. What say you to all of this, you adorable little bundle of joy?"

Although I was only nine weeks old, anyone with feeling recognizes love for the valuable gift it is. So I looked up at Ma, yapped at her in an attempt to let her know that I too warmed to her, and when she brought me up to her cheek for an even more heartfelt cuddle, I snuggled right in there as if I had been doing it long before now.

"I think I'm in love," Ma said to Pa, who now started to organize our departure with the gamekeeper.

We were duly loaded into the back of the Mercedes estate car after they had spread a thick layer of newspaper in the back to soak up any "accidents", as they referred to our functions of nature, and then we were shooting off into the countryside for the journey south to London.

Having never been in a car before, we puppies were not exactly enamoured of the rocking motion of the moving vehicle, but we took our cue from Sootie, who was lying down contentedly - doubtless ticking off the miles until she had returned home to Kensington – and before long we had all settled down as the Mercedes sped southwards down the motorway.

Six hours later, the car came to a smooth halt. Arising from a deep slumber, I saw that we were parked outside a cream coloured house in what I would subsequently come to know as the Belgravia district of London. Pa flipped open the back door, reached in and plucked me up before I even had time to react. "Time to say good-bye to Tum Tum, Sootie," he said, and with those words, handed me over to Ma.

Ma must have thought that Sootie was looking sad for she said, "Don't worry, Sootie. You'll see Tum Tum tomorrow morning when we go for our morning run."

Ma gave her a gentle pat, Pa shut the car door, and before I could even figure out what was happening, Pa was giving Ma a peck on the cheek while also opening the front door of the house for her.

"See you in the morning," they said to each other as Ma turned on the entrance hall light prior to shutting the door behind us.

I felt my heart leap. Where was I? What was this strange place, with that peculiar patterned thing on the wall which I would soon learn was called wallpaper? It was all very well for this nice but strange lady to be cradling me in her arms. But why was I here? Why wasn't I curled up against Sootie's ample tummy?

Ma took me up to the second floor and opened the door to yet another strange set of rooms. "Well, Tum Tum, we're home," she said in a tone of voice that was entirely too cheerful for my liking. She put me down onto the grey carpet and said, "You go explore while I fix you some supper." And with that she left me to 'explore'.

And explore I did. There was a plethora of new scents and sights to come to terms with. All very different from what I was used to. As I sniffed my way around, I wasn't at all sure that I would like this place. It was all so new. So different so *clean*. In an attempt to make it more familiar, I started to lay down a marker of my own. As I squatted and felt the warmth of my urine trickle down on to the floor, I was interrupted. "No, no. Not there, Tum Tum. Good girls do their pees on the newspaper, on the grass or in the street," Ma scolded. "Here, darling," she said, her voice softening as she bent down to scoop me up, urine still trickling down from my opened bladder, "Let's go find the newspaper."

The Sunday Times was neatly laid down in the kitchen, a few feet away from a water bowl. That I recognized, for we had water bowls in Scotland. Food bowls too. Mine was on the kitchen counter, full to overflowing from a tin of puppy food open beside it. My nostrils twitched in anticipation. I could already taste dinner, which of course was the same food that the gamekeeper had been feeding me. Ma and Pa were nothing if not thorough and considerate.

"This is where you must do your business when you feel like it. Not on the carpet. Okay?" Ma said, plonking me down on the newspaper to reinforce the message. She then reached for the bowl of food and placed it beside the water bowl.

Needless to say, I dug right in and wolfed down my supper. All that travelling had left me famished.

When I had finished, Ma said, "You look as if you could do with some more. I know your Pa said I shouldn't feed you too much, but maybe just this once I'll give you seconds." With which she spooned half the remnants of the tin into my food bowl.

This strange lady seemed so keen to be loving and reasonable that I decided then and there I'd humour her. So, as soon as I had finished eating, I headed for the newspaper, squatted, took a tiny piddle, while shooting her a look as if to say, Right you are. Lo and behold, she understood, for she said, "You are a clever one, aren't you? Unless I'm very much mistaken, that was as firm an assent of understanding as I've ever witnessed."

With that, Ma scooped me up into her arms, said, "Come, let me give you a guided tour of your new home," and started to tell me what each room was; what I could do; what I could not; all the while speaking to me as if I understood every word. The problem was, she was using words I'd never heard before. Things like drawing room, bedroom, bathroom, sofas were as alien to me as the concept of a walk in the park or holding my business in until I was on the grass, though I had got the message about the newspaper.

Although I didn't understand half of what Ma was saying, I resolved then and there to do my best to meet her half way. Like most other spaniels, I instinctively understood that co-operation and

Even authentic love-children take awhile to train their parents, as I found to my cost.

consideration are the basis of a good relationship, and I could sense that this was what Ma wanted us to have. I therefore looked her straight in the eye, yelped my willingness to be a good and loving girl, licked her hand in visible proof thereof, and snuggled up to her even more than I had been doing so far. "I do declare, you're trying to tell me that you might not yet understand everything I'm saying, but you're going to make a real effort to oblige me nevertheless," she said so heartfeltedly that I couldn't help melting a little more.

We finished our spin round my new home in the very room we had started out from: the kitchen. Ma was clearly intent on laying down some ground rules up front, for she pointed to a wicker basket lined with a fitted cushion in the corner near to the refrigerator, "Tum Tum, just as how you're not allowed onto the sofas in the sitting room, nor onto the bed in my bedroom, I'm not allowed into your basket. Only you are allowed into your basket. It's for you and you alone, unless, of course, you want to invite another dog to share it with you. Like Sootie, for instance. Each of us has our own territory, and we must respect each other's, OK?"

Territory is a word which dogs understand no matter what language the word is in. Having got the message, I headed towards the newspaper to do another pee. "Good girl," Ma said, and, as soon as I had finished, she scooped me up. She started to mess with my neck, putting a contraption around it which she called a collar – very odd feeling, I can tell you, though I soon got used to it – and without more ado attached a thing she described as a lead to it. When she had finished, she said with brisk satisfaction, "Time for walkies. I bet you don't know what walkies are yet. But you will. I promise you, you will. Walkies are what all grown-up doggies save up their pees and poohs for." And with that most perplexing explanation – which of course I would understand the meaning of only too well in the not too distant future – Ma and I set off for a walk up West Eaton Place to Eaton Square.

That first urban peregrination had to be one of the most challenging events of my whole life. I was positively bombarded by strange sights and smells. Some human. Some plant. And many animal. It had never occurred to me before that there could be so many different dogs in the world, much less other animals, all of whom were laying down their markers in the form of urine with bewildering multiplicity alongside the kerbs, lamp posts, and trees of this London city street. By the time I was trying to squirt the twelfth lamp post with the pathetic little tinkle remaining to me, I was regretting having wasted such a precious commodity on the Sunday Times in Ma's flat. Clearly, what Ma was trying to tell me, about saving up my pees, now made sense, though she hadn't explained it properly, telling me about being a good girl when really the point was that I needed every bit of that liquid to make my mark in the world at large. Plainly, the newspaper was for when I was in danger of having an accident. But, if London demanded as much urine as I suspected it would in future, I couldn't afford to have accidents in the flat, otherwise I would be squandering a valuable resource that I definitely needed if I was going to have any impact at all upon this great metropolis.

On the way back to the flat, I had my first experience of a fundamental difference between humankind and beast. Ma started to get impatient with me because I was stopping every time I smelt another dog's marker and tried my level best to dribble out a bit of my own. Quite unable to understand the importance of what I was doing, she said, "Enough, Tum Tum, You'll just have to wait till later," as if deferred endeavour were preferable to immediate enterprise. She then pressed a button and my lead retracted so dramatically that I was no longer able to gad about at will, but had to totter alongside her ankle. How, I wondered, had she done that?

I can't say the view of the world is so great with an ankle included in one's peripheral vision, but that method of walking certainly proved to be expeditious in getting us back home at a speed which squandered many an opportunity for a good sniff and squirt.

Even though I found this method wasteful, Ma seemed very pleased with both me and herself. "Aren't you a good girl," she said as we were approaching our front door. "Walking to heel as if it were second nature. Well done, Tum Tum. I can already see that you are a good girl and we are going to get along just fine."

Once back home, she turned on the television in her bedroom. She lay on her bed, so naturally I tried to get in beside her. But she wasn't having any of it, and informed me that I mustn't climb up on the bed, but should watch television "down there," patting an area beside the bed.

All dogs know that there is very little point in humans having pets if we can't snuggle up to them. Both they and we lose so many benefits unless we are able to have a truly good cuddle. While the odd dog-lover is deluded about the benefits of what they term boundaries and cleanliness, more sensible personalities can hurtle inadvertently into those pitfalls as well, under the mistaken belief that a well-behaved pet must live at floor level.

Unfortunately, Ma was headed down that mistaken pathway. What is a nine week old puppy to do? How can we demonstrate the error of their ways? Especially when we are new to our human mother and she is an unknown to us as well? So I picked up on the vibe and lay my little head down on my little paw on the floor beside the bed, taking good care to stay as close to her as possible.

That, it turned out, was a clever move. Within moments, Ma's hand had travelled downwards and she was stroking me gently on my back, her fingers moving back and forth, back and forth. I was soon suffused with contentment, and found myself drifting off to a sleep.

I awoke with a start. "Time for good-night walkies, Tum Tum," Ma was saying as she bent down to pick me up.

Yikes, I thought. I've only just got to sleep and already I have to go outside for more walkies. I can tell you, at that moment, I wasn't at all sure I would like this new way of life at all. In Scotland, we had only gone out for walkies occasionally. The rest of the time, we had stayed nicely tucked up in our straw-strewn stall in the kennels, luxuriating with each other – each other being my siblings and Sootie. Still, I wasn't about to surrender to dispiritedness so easily, so I licked Ma's hand as she picked up me up to attach the lead to my collar, then I bounded down the stairs with her into the darkness.

If Ma wanted me nice and rested for the night, she was certainly going about it in a paradoxical manner. Once I sniffed the brisk night air along with the myriad scents on offer, I was hyper-alert, and promptly started to tug at my lead. "No, no, Tum Tum," Ma said. "You mustn't pull away like that. Come to heel, darling," she said, once more reeling me in like a fish caught on the River Test.

I must tell you, I didn't like this heel business at all, but soon Ma got fed up with what she called my agitation, and released the lead "this once". Victory. I was off, sniffing and squirting for all my miniscule life was worth, until Ma declared after a walk around the block that we had had "enough for one night", and led me back upstairs to the place she called "home".

I could hardly believe it when she led me into the kitchen and put me to lie down in the basket. "This is where you sleep, Tum Tum," she said, bending down to stroke me.

Naturally, I started to lick her hands and moved out of the basket, so that I could get closer to her to give her a proper cuddle.

"No. No," she said. "You mustn't leave your basket. Come, let me put you back," she said, picking me up and giving me a juicy kiss and delicious cuddle before replacing me in the basket.

No sooner did she do that than she turned heel, turned off the light, and was out of the room before I had a chance to catch my bearings, much less proffer all the licks all over her cheeks and lips I just knew she would love to have. Reality now imposed itself upon me in a wholly unwelcome way. I could hardly believe how cruel fate was being. Was I really expected to spend a whole night all alone, with no one to cuddle with? No one to give love to, or receive it from? Wasn't it bad enough that I was making the adjustment from my canine mother to my human one? Was I now supposed to go against nature and ignore my gift for loving as well?

I tried to be brave, to get to sleep without the sweet sensation of another body next to mine, but no matter how much I wanted to be a good girl or how hard I tried to exercise courage, I simply could not get past the terrible loneliness I felt. Though I tried not to cry, I couldn't help it. Slowly and quietly, the whimpers started to escape from me. Ma must have heard them, for she came back into the kitchen, turned on the light, bent down to pat me, and said, "I know, darling. It's very difficult for you. You've never slept alone before. But you'll soon be used to it. Here. Let me give you some cuddles." With which she started to stroke me, holding me securely so that I could not leap up into her lap as my impulses dictated I do, until I relaxed and was calm again.

Incredible as it may sound, that was her signal to get up, turn the light off again, and was once more, abandon me to my lonely fate – a fate she was also condemning herself to in her bedroom.

This time I didn't even bother to try to adjust to such a crazy scenario. As wave after wave of loneliness engulfed me, I gave way to whimpers first, and then howls.

After a few minutes, I heard Ma shout out, "Tum Tum, you've got to be quiet. I am not coming for you, so you may as well get used to the fact that you will be sleeping alone."

Could humans really be so out of touch with the natural order that they would opt for icy loneliness rather than warm and loving companionability? I simply could not get my heart around such a self-defeating notion, and though I realized that Ma wanted me to be stop my howls of anguish, I could not.

With the wisdom of hindsight, I can now see I was caught up in a fundamental struggle that many other living creatures experience. On the one hand there was my natural inclination to give and receive love, and on the other was my desire to please my new mother, even when doing so went against the grain. Being so young, I was not yet properly trained, nor could I control my natural tendencies, and I therefore had to articulate the most dreadful maelstrom of grief, loneliness, and frustration that were overwhelming me.

Everyone knows how they feel when they have been abandoned to a cruel fate. Not only do you feel bereft, but you also lose all sense of time. Or, to put it another way, time assumes another dimension, and stretches out almost into timelessness. I therefore had absolutely no idea how long my agony went on for, but I do know exactly when it ended. Suddenly, the light was on and Ma was standing over me, her expression a combination of concern – whose fragrance I could also pick up quite separately - as well as annoyance. The advantage of being a spaniel, of course, is that I could discern, even at my tender age, that the levels of concern which she was emanating were considerably stronger than the whiffs of annoyance, though quite how I could capitalize upon that knowledge was something I could not fathom.

Fortunately for me, I didn't have to do a thing. Ma walked over to my basket, bent over it, picked me up, and said, "I suppose it is cruel to expect a tiny puppy like you to sleep alone on your first night away from your mother. So let's go into the bedroom. You can sleep beside the bed."

She went to the linen cupboard, took out a towel, spread it on the floor beside the bed, and put me on it. "There," she said, gently stroking me. "That will be better. Now go to sleep."

She got into bed, her head no more than a foot or two away from mine, and turned out the light.

I cannot tell you how embarrassed I was when I started to whimper again. The thought of this nice, kind, sweet new mother such a short distance away from me, with neither of us being able to enjoy the benefit of cuddling – two feet or two hundred feet is still a gap that denies all comfort – was too much to bear.

"There, there, you go to sleep now," Ma said as she bent down to stroke me. Naturally, I calmed down immediately, but when she stopped and the cold blast of that two foot gap chilled my soul again, I once more started to whimper. So Ma stroked me again. This time, however, the urge to cuddle became so overpowering that I jumped up on to the bed and snuggled into her tummy.

"I don't think so," Ma said, laughing, and put me down on to the towel again.

She stroked me some more, then, thinking I should be asleep, she stopped. The temptation of having this loving, cuddlesome being so near to me once more overwhelmed me and I started to whimper again.

"OK, Tum Tum. You win. You can sleep with me tonight. Just this once. That will give you a chance to get used to being away from Sootie. But tomorrow night you'll have to sleep in your basket."

Ma lifted me into the bed and I snuggled by her bosom, my head neatly fitting under her chin. The bliss of that lovely warm body next to mine compelled me to lick her, and before I knew what was happening, I was drifting off to a deep and satisfying sleep.

Fortunately for both Ma and me, tomorrow never came. For the remainder of my life, we slept together, giving each other the love we needed, and receiving the love each of us had to give. And love, let's face facts, is life's greatest gift.

Chapter Three

"I often felt lonely before I got Tum Tum, but since she came into my life, I have never again felt lonely. Not even once," Ma used to say, and I daresay it was true.

After the hiatus of that first night's false start, Ma and I "bonded", to employ the vernacular so popular with humans nowadays, with a speed that opened up both our hearts and lives. And yet we came perilously close to losing each other.

The misadventure began simply enough, the first morning I was with her in London.

She woke me up at 6:35, announcing that we were going to meet Pa, Sootie and my siblings for a run in the park. Although I had no concept of what runs in the park were, I was already happy to give her my trust, for I could tell it would not be misplaced. So I jumped down from our bed and allowed her to attach me to my lead.

After a short stop outside the house to lighten my bladder, she walked me to her red Renault, opened the door, and was in the process of putting me in it when I clambered up and settled myself on the seat beside hers. "My goodness, what a clever girl you are," she exclaimed, as if I were doing something exceptional, when all I was doing was being a sensible dog and taking the seat beside hers. As I could tell which one was hers simply from the scent remaining on it, this was

Here I am on the bed that I wasn't supposed to be on EVER.

hardly rocket science, though she seemed to think it was.

She gunned the engine and announced that we were off to Hyde Park. The journey could have taken no more than five or so minutes, during which I was riveted by the multiplicity of sights, scents and sounds that whizzed by us. If a walk around Eaton Square had been amazing, this array of offerings was beyond description. London, I could already tell, was definitely stimulating, and later on I could well see why Samuel Johnson had said that he "who is tired of London is tired of life".

Only too soon, Ma and I were pulling in to the parking lot of a place I would come to know well: the Royal Albert Hall. As we did so, Pa, Sootie and the other puppies also pulled in, in their car. After parking side by side, Ma and Pa got all the puppies on leads, and it was then that I noticed that two of my siblings were missing. Looking around for them, I heard Pa telling Ma that some friends of his had taken them.

Now, it is quite wrong of human beings to think that dogs don't feel the wrench of separation from our pack. Of course we do. Just because we instinctively know that we will rejoin our loved ones in Pet Heaven, which makes us stalwart, doesn't mean that we are unfeeling. But we are fortunate enough to be blessed with good powers of recuperation as well as innate equanimity. These allow us to make the painful transition without significantly reducing our capacity for love, trust and substitution.

We are also able to make strong and lasting bonds quickly, which I was soon to find out to my cost.

The problem started once Pa had us on the grass beside the Albert Memorial in the park. He undid all our leads over Ma's protestations. She was worried we might run away or get lost, but he brushed her concerns aside, telling her there was "nothing to worry about and they have to learn to stick together without leads, so they may as well start now." I could tell by the hang-dog expression on her face that Ma was not convinced, but she fell into line with the rest of us and, after we had all done our business, away we went, running around the park in hot pursuit of Pa, Ma and Sootie.

It was amazing how unified we all were, when you stop to consider that this was the first time any of us puppies had been for a run together, much less one in London's most popular park. I suppose what aided the endeavour was that we were pretty much the only people in the park at that time of the day. This lessened distractions, though I cannot say it eliminated them entirely, for the circuit was a wealth of scents related to quantities of dogs, squirrels, horses, even ducks that had left their marks there, not to mention the flora and fauna which proliferated everywhere. But Pa set a firm if gentle pace which brooked neither opposition nor interference, and as the momentum sped us along, we all happily ran as one.

Only when the Albert Memorial loomed into view did Pa loosen the pace. By the time we were in Prince Albert's shadow, he and Ma had come to a full stop and he was bending down to attach our leads. Briskly.

"There we go," he said to Ma, handing her one of the leads.

"Let me check to be sure that it's Tum Tum," she said, mindful that my brother and I looked uncannily alike.

"Don't be such a fuss budget," Pa remonstrated. "Of course it's Tum Tum. Do you think I can't tell the difference between our lovechild and her brother?" He bent over, pecked Ma on the cheek and before she even had a chance to think much less respond, he had shot off with Sootie, me and the other puppies in tow to the strains of,

"Mustn't be late for work. See you later, darling."

Without a moment's hesitation, Pa ran towards Kensington Road, and, there being no traffic coming in either direction, ran across the road towards the parking lot opposite with all of us in tow. No sooner did we reach the Mercedes Benz than he had the back door open and was bundling us inside.

Knowing only too well that something was wrong, I looked through the back window as Ma loomed into view waving frantically. But Pa was already turning the car onto the road, oblivious to her presence or the patent panic in her gestures.

"What is going on now?" I asked Sootie. "I thought I was going to be Ma's new baby?"

"Pa has mixed you up," she said. "Don't worry. I'm sure he'll straighten everything out once he gets us home."

"Are you really sure? I love Ma already and I wouldn't want to be without her."

"Don't worry," Sootie said. "Just come and snuggle close to me until they have a chance to untangle the mess."

Sootie's confidence, however, was sorely misplaced, for no sooner did Pa get us back to his house than he was on the phone arranging to have me - or rather the brother with whom he had confused me – picked up by his new owners.

"Ten o'clock then," I heard him say at the conclusion of the call, as I edged right into Sootie's rib cage in an attempt to gain some comfort.

Pa, I was learning to my cost, was one of those Scotsmen for whom the word brisk could have been invented. No sooner did he hang up than he went straight upstairs to have his shower. As luck would have it, he turned on the water at the precise moment that Ma telephoned. I can still hear the ringing sound in my ears and feel Sootie shrinking disconsolately into the edge of her basket when Pa's voice came on the answering machine asking callers to leave a message. Sootkins knew our Pa so well that she was aware that he would walk out of the house without even looking to see if anyone had called.

At ten o'clock, the housekeeper let in a strange man, who stooped down to pick me up even though I was yelping my protests while Sootie was growling in protestation at the error he was making. "You hold her collar," he instructed the housekeeper, pointing to Sootie, "and keep her still by twisting it if necessary. We don't want her biting either of us."

While Sootie struggled for breath, he quickly scooped me up and was out the front door and headed down Pembroke Road in the direction of his car and driver, parked with the engine running for a fast getaway. He jumped into the back seat with me, ordered the driver to return to his house on Holland Park Avenue, and turned me over to inspect me as if I were a piece of meat in a butcher's shop. Thank God. For it was then that he noticed that I was not the male that he wanted, but a definite female.

By this time, Ma had been leaving every-increasingly frantic messages with Pa's secretary, but in those pre-mobile telephone days, there was precious little she could do to reach him. He was between appointments in the City (as they all called the Square Mile known otherwise as the City of London) where he had his stockbrokerage firm. Fortunately one of the secretaries managed to waylay him at about eleven o'clock and tell him about the mix-up. Two quick telephone calls later and everything was straightened out. I would be returned to Ma by my chauffeur-driven kidnapper, and my brother would be restored to his rightful owner, who had a shoot in Hampshire and wanted him to be trained as his gundog.

Of course, I knew nothing about this arrangement as I lay in my brother's basket in the morning room, rueing the horror of having met and lost my Ma. All I knew was that I did not like my kidnapper at all. He gave off no waves of love, at least not for me, though when he took me back to Ma's house later that morning, I could smell his pores open up a bit for Jeremy, as he called my look-alike sibling, after he had concluded a successful genital inspection.

They say that all is well that ends well, and I suppose it is. But I can tell you the shock of being separated affected both Ma and me so much that we were both extra careful to stay together thereafter. It was a salutary lesson, but we learnt it well. Ma always kept me on a leash whenever we were outside, the only exception being when we went to the park. Even then, she was careful to keep me within sight of her, at least until she adjudged me properly trained, which was when I was about six months old, even though I had poohs, pees, sitting, standing, staying, and fetching down pat long before that – in fact, within a matter of weeks of being with Ma I could even sit upright and proffer my right paw for guests to shake it.

For my first five months with Ma, we lived a block away from Eaton Square in West Eaton Place. Ma often went out at night. Although she always came back at what she called a 'civilized' hour, I would have to face four or five or sometimes even six hours on my own. I can assure you that was pure torment for me. Dogs being sociable by nature, we absolutely loathe being left alone. Of course, if we have other dogs for company, that makes being left more bearable, but even then, what we really need is having the leader of our pack present, which is what our Ma or Pa are.

I used to bark and bark and bark in protest when Ma was out wining and dining, but since we lived alone in the house, no one was there to be disturbed and complain to her about the noise. Then my luck changed. One day one of the neighbours, who usually lived in the country but was spending some rare time at his house in London opposite ours, complained that I had been disturbing him the night before. He told Ma that he was having an important dinner party that same evening, and could she please ensure that my barking did not ruin it for his guests if she was not going to be at home.

"I am so sorry. I had no idea Tum Tum barked when I'm out," she said. You could tell she was embarrassed, not only by the register of her voice but also by the scent she was giving off and the flat expression on her normally-animated face.

No sooner were we on our own than she said, "Well, Tum Tum, I suppose we'll have to take you with us this evening and leave you in the car. Will you like it at night the way you do during the day?"

Naturally, I responded with yelps of delight.

"You are telling me you'd like that, aren't you?" Ma said. To reinforce my message, I jumped up onto her and started to paw her insistently. Even though she disliked it when I sprang like the springer

I was, this affirmed my message in a way nothing else could. To soften the effect, however, I also unleashed my tongue and gave her as many slobbering licks as I could manage in the shortest space of time.

Ma responded by laughing delightedly and pushing me away with a degree of mock annoyance that also contained a kernel of the genuine article. "Okay, okay. I've got the message." With which she placed by two front paws very firmly on the ground and reminded me yet again that good girls don't jump up.

It's not possible for doggies to change mood as suddenly as human sometimes want us to, and as I stayed at floor level, my body enacted its own dance of pleasure. My tail wagged along with my buttocks, my spine twisting from side to side as I gave physical expression to what was going on in my heart.

Ma was right there on my wavelength, for she continued to laugh and said, "Tonight you come with us and stay in the car. Thrillsville."

By this time, Ma and I had settled into a daily routine. She already knew that I liked being taken out and left in the car, just as how I knew she truly enjoyed my company, for she would take me everywhere she could.

In those days the London department stores still allowed shoppers' pets to accompany them, so I got to know both Peter Jones and Harrods pretty well. We were also allowed to travel on the tube, and while I hated the escalator and resolutely refused to step on it – forcing Ma to pick me up in her arms – on the few occasions that she had reason to take the tube she took me along with her and I did enjoy the hustle and bustle of the train-ride as long as the carriage wasn't too full. If it was, I tucked myself beneath her seat so that the other passengers couldn't step on my paws inadvertently, but even that prospect couldn't entirely negate the pleasure of being in such a stimulating environment.

Dogs couldn't go into supermarkets, but that didn't stop Ma taking me along for the ride and leaving me in the car with the window cracked open a few inches for fresh air. Restaurants in town were a bit trickier. While the odd one in the country allowed in dogs, none in London did, so Ma would leave me at home when she went out for dinner, hence how the problem with the neighbour arose.

I hated being left alone in the house. It was dull and boring and so unsociable. Quite unlike being left in the car, where I had a ringside seat of the evolving parade that was London life, especially if she had parked on the street instead of in a parking lot or parking garage.

By this time, Ma and I had developed a rather pleasing routine that suited both of us. After our morning run, we returned home. She fed me, bathed and dressed herself for the day, then either went out (with me in tow) to play tennis (tethering me to a bench unless the courts were enclosed, in which case she allowed me to sit on the sidelines), or she stayed at home and wrote, with me resting behind her chair. We would break after a couple of hours for her to take me for a quick walk, which was inevitably followed by the welcome announcement, "bickies in basket". This was my cue to rush into my basket to await a handful of biscuits. For some reason, this always made Ma laugh joyously. Afterwards, I would bask in her approval while sitting and watching her eat her lunch and read the newspapers. This was always followed by a quick spin around the block before returning home to write some more while I again rested at her feet or in my basket.

At around four o'clock, Ma would change into her exercise clothes, which was always the precursor to us going for another quick walk followed by a drive to her health club. While she was inside doing aerobics, I was outside in the car watching the world go by. I could happily sit for hours on end, enjoying the passing delights, a deep bowl of water on the floor behind the passenger seat in case I got thirsty.

Sometimes, passersby would stop to admire me and occasionally to check on me. Of course, I always went right up to them and licked their fingers if they tried to push them through the gap between the top of the window and the door frame. Some of those exchanges were pretty heart-warming, I can tell you. I often had the impression that the English truly are a nation of dog-lovers, though I did not like it quite so much when the odd eccentric would try to establish an intense relationship through the glass in the mistaken belief that I had spent my whole life waiting for them to come along and amuse me. At times like those, I would accommodate them until they crossed over into an excess of misguided intrusiveness. Then I would withdraw without either a snarl or a growl by turning tail and jumping up onto the ledge between the back window and the back seat. Once there, I would position myself in such a way that I was able to gaze at them serenely. From that safe distance, I could observe their kind-hearted albeit misplaced antics until they realized that they should go about their business and leave me to mine. Which was the comfortable enjoyment of the whole array of delectables, whose very transience partaken of with comfortable remoteness was what made the every-changing feast such an enjoyable banquet of sensual delights.

Life would have been ideal if Ma had not got into the habit of leaving me alone when she went out in the evening. But now that our neighbour had complained about my barking, and she had decided to take me with her that night, I had hopes of us establishing a new routine.

Certainly, things began well enough. She parked our car on Pall Mall while she went into one of those palatial clubs where friends of hers were holding a dance, leaving me to while away the hours happily as I looked at people coming and going. This new arrangement sure beat being left alone at West Eaton Place, I can tell you.

Later on, when Ma returned to the car and we set off back home, I yapped away, telling her how much I had enjoyed myself and how I hoped this was the beginning of a new and far more interesting regimen than her previous one of leaving me in enforced isolation at home.

You can imagine my consternation when I discovered the following evening that she was going out and planning to leave me at home alone, in keeping with the old routine. Last night had not been the start of a new order. It had been an aberration. A sop to our neighbour.

I started to bark my protests. At first, Ma thought I was being my customarily sweet and friendly self. Misjudging the mood completely, she responded with such inappropriate comments as, "And what interesting morsel are you trying to dish up for me, you darling baby love?" This forced me to intensify my yapping, and while that grabbed her attention and made her realize that all was not well in the land of the loving, she still had not got the message, for she kept on asking silly questions such as, "And what are you trying to tell me, Tum Tum? Are you hungry? Do you want to go back outside?" When she knew very well that we had just come in from a walk.

In desperation, I jumped up on the bed, barked very firmly and growled as darkly as I could. Because I had never actually done that to her before, it caught her attention. She looked at me quizzically. I looked at her directly. Having made eye to eye contact, I held her gaze long enough for her to say, "You are definitely trying to tell me something. What is it?"

Yapping and yelping and growling having failed, I decided to issue as personal a message as I could muster. So I got up off my haunches, bent my back legs so that I squatted, and peed right in the bed. Our bed.

Ma's response was instantaneous. Irate at what she misconstrued as my naughtiness, she smacked me squarely on the bottom with her open palm, before taking me outside and giving me a lecture about how good girls do their business outside while bad girls do it inside. But the worst girls of all do it on the bed.

Let me tell you, training human beings can be a real grind. Not only do they frequently fail to get the message, but they even punish us for their lack of comprehension. However, persistence wins the day.

The following evening, when Ma was reaching the end of the titivation process which always preceded her abandoning me to my lonely fate while she was out and about gallivanting, I again started to bark my protests. I was determined that I would make her understand that I wanted her to take me with her and leave me in the car, instead of marooning me for several hours of boring solitude. Once more, I hopped onto the bed. This time I planted myself with even more resolve than the night before. As I barked and barked and barked, Ma said, "You're telling me you don't want to be left here, aren't you? But I can't take you with me every time I go out. You'll just have to get used to being here on your own some of the time."

We'll see about that, I thought. I once more growled in protest. This again captured Ma's attention the way it had the night before. As our eyes locked, I looked directly at her in the hope that my most plaintive look would soften her, but when I saw she intended to remain unbending, I threw caution to the winds. Maintaining eye contact, I arched my back and proceeded to make the most substantial protest I could engineer. This took the form of a nice, thick, solid pooh, delivered fair and square in the centre of the bed. As I did so, Ma did a fair imitation of Vesuvius, erupting furiously and berating me for making her have to change the sheets two nights running. But this time I got through to her, for when she had calmed down, she said, "I suppose if you hate being left along to such an extent that you will defile your own bed, you leave me with no option but to take you with me when I go out. So Tum Tum, you win. Congratulations."

From then until my (human) brothers were born eight years later, and I could be left with them and their nanny while Ma was out on the town without succumbing to boredom or loneliness, I invariably accompanied her on her nightly peregrinations. Whether she was going to dinner, to a drinks party, a vernissage, a ball, or a concert, I went too. On only one occasion did she deviate from that most sensible routine, but I shall save my account of it for later, as it reflects so well upon the Police that it would be a shame to tell the tale out of sequence.

Once I had cracked that nut with Ma, we got along so well that you could almost have said that we had a perfect understanding. I say almost, because there was one significant area where our approaches were so diametrically opposed that we might well have fallen out over our differences, had we not shared spaniel-like dispositions.

Food was the bone of contention. Ma had this very human approach which required regular feeding of set portions. And not only for me, but for her own self and her friends as well. Although her friend Kate used to say that she liked coming to dinner at our house because Ma was the only hostess in 1980s London who served sensible traditional fare in boarding school-sized helpings instead of the *nouvelle cuisine* snippets that were all the rage at the time, Ma was a great one for moderation. "The world would be a far better place if people appreciated the value of sufficiency," was one of her guiding precepts, but since that was at variance with the fact that most Springer Spaniels will eat until they burst rather than leave food uneaten – and I was definitely one of the greedier members of our breed - it was only a matter of time before our different attitudes brought us into conflict.

I have to chuckle to myself as I look back at the very first occasion we nearly came to blows. I was six months old and well on my way to being my full height, if not weight. Although Ma used to have at least one dinner party a week, I could tell that this one was special because of the trouble she was going to. First we went shopping at Portobello Market for her to get fresh tomatoes and mandarin oranges for the soup as well as fresh broccoli and even newly-slaughtered pork for the main course. Then we stopped off at Harrod's Food Hall where she bought a full Brie which had me salivating almost painfully as I accompanied her on the walk back to the car, my nose nestling beside the green shopping bag. After we had wound our way through the Perfumery Hall - that vast series of rooms which house every perfume known to woman in the Western World - not even the pungent scents from that riot of fragrances could deflect my attention from the overwhelming attractions of that most delectable-smelling French cheese. So I gave way to temptation and burrowed my snout into the bag. I must have got carried away, for Ma suddenly jerked my leash, said, "Behave yourself, Tum Tum. That Brie is for my guests, not you," and moved it from her right hand to her left, where it remained, a safe distance separating us, until we reached the car.

Any hopes I had of being reunited with that cheese were dashed when Ma put it into the boot along with the other food. But time was on my side, for when we returned to the house and she had unloaded all the shopping, she left the Brie on top of the small refrigerator to 'breathe'- quite forgetting that I could reach it.

Thereafter, for the rest of the afternoon, Ma was a veritable tornado of activity as she fixed flowers, cooked, set the table, lit the gas fire in the sitting room, put sandalwood scent in the lamp burners, prior to bathing and dressing to receive her guests.

It was while she was combing her hair that I succumbed to temptation. I was in the kitchen drinking water when I realized that I had a good ten or so minutes to myself. I ask you, what would you do if you were in my paws? Quite so. You'd do exactly as I did. Go to the refrigerator and take a really good sniff of the Brie that had been haunting my nostrils all afternoon with its succulence.

There is a reason why the Lord's Prayer requests "lead us not into temptation". Temptation laid down before us can be irresistible, as I was just about to discover. Even though I knew only too well that Ma had bought the source of my downfall for her guests and not for me, four hours of temptation finally became too much to resist, and no sooner did I bury my nose in the drooling side of that soft cheese than I became incapable of further resistance. As I felt that soft substance nestle near my nostrils and its delicious scents wafted their way down my airways, I confess I was overwhelmed. With nary a thought for whether Ma would be cross, or even whether so much of a good thing would prove to be my undoing in more ways than one, I nudged temptation from the top of the refrigerator to the ground with one almighty heave.

Having dislodged this heavenly substance to a more accessible place, I wolfed it down in five efficient gulps. Millions of years of evolution having taught us doggies not to hang about and munch our way through meals the way the French do, not when there is every possibility that someone or something will come along to whip our treat away from us, I reverted to animal precision. And, knowing only too well what Ma would have done as certainly as any other beast of the field if she had caught me; I gave way to a more leisurely pace only after the main body of the Brie was safely inside my own.

Humans may think that they are the only beings whose meals are broken up into different courses. This, however, is one of the many misnomers to which homo sapiens falls prey in the mistaken belief that they are so much better than other animals that they do things entirely differently, when in fact many of their habits are simply variations of our own. In fact, most animals' meals have different sections which are equivalent to the various courses humans have. With us doggies, it is a matter of gulping followed by savouring. So no sooner did I finish devouring most of the Brie than I changed pace and turned my attention to licking up each and every bit that remained on the floor. Doing so at a more leisurely pace, I savoured the taste and scents in a manner that was almost as intent as bourgeois ladies in Paris rotating the few morsels of cheese and dessert (or anything else fattening for that matter) that they allow themselves as they struggle to maintain the conflicting balance between retention of a slim figure and enjoyment of the delights of the table.

Only when I had exhausted every last scent and taste did I raise my head and start to sniff to discern where Ma was. It took no more than two or three quick drags of the air to learn that she was still in the bathroom, putting the final touches to her coiffeur with the hairspray whose sweetness always drifted throughout the rooms on that floor with the exactitude of a road map.

Of course, I had an idea how Ma would react once she discovered what I had done, for, even though I had never eaten a whole cheese before, I had swiped the odd bit of food here and there. Always, Ma remonstrated, ordering me to "get down", to "behave" myself, and even sometimes to "stop being such a greedy guts", invariably followed by the refrain, "When I named you, I had no idea I was choosing your primary obsession." I wasn't naïve enough to think she would be pleased when she found out, so I decided to work my brains and promptly sauntered into the bedroom and settled down onto the bed, a veritable picture of innocence and contentment, knowing very well that she would soon come back into the bedroom to put on her jewellery.

I must confess to feeling slightly cloyed as I waited for her to finish whatever it was she was doing in the bathroom. All that dairy wasn't lying as easily on my tum tum as I had hoped it would, but if I was paying the price for my indulgence, it had also been worth it, for it had been truly delectable in terms of both taste and scent.

As I had anticipated, within a matter of minutes, Ma came into the bedroom. She stroked me lightly, as was her wont whenever she walked past me. She went to the chest of drawers and opened up her jewellery box. "Tum Tum, the harbingers for this evening have been so positive that I'm almost floating on air. It's seldom that everything falls into place so easily that one wonders if a guardian angel isn't directing things from the great unseen," she announced.

My sentiments exactly. So I gave her one of my soulful looks.

Because we dogs live in the moment far more fully than human beings do, I had already forgotten that I had consumed her entire cheese course. As she bent down and kissed me between the eyes, she said, "I know I keep on saying so, but I really do have to thank God for having brought you into my life. You are such a joy. Come. Let's go for a quick spin around the block before everyone comes."

Fortunately, I was not the only person who had forgotten about the Brie. It had obviously fallen off Ma's radar as well, for, when we returned from our walk and went into the kitchen for her to carve the pork after giving me 'bickies in basket' she took out the roasting tray, put it on top of the refrigerator, and happily carved away as if that space was supposed to be blank.

From then until it was time for the cheese course, Ma acted as if the Brie had never existed. She used, reused, and disused that refrigerator top as if she had never had anything edible on it. Then, after she had served the pudding, she spun around, reached for the Brie, realized it was not there – and had not been for hours – and declared, as if she were Demosthenes and I one of the crowd in an Ancient Greek stadium, "I don't believe it. Tum Tum. You've eaten the cheese. A whole cheese. How could you! You are a naughty girl. Naughty."

The reaction she received, however, was not what she would have expected. One of the guests, a fat and nice man named Henry whom I had never met before but who was obviously the guest of honour, for he was seated at Ma's right, laughed loudly and said, "Who's a clever girl, then. I'd eat a whole Brie if someone left it out for me."

That set everyone off laughing. Even Ma was tinkling, though that usually meant that she was aspiring to amusement rather than experiencing it. Nevertheless, this laughter stopped me in my tracks. I had scarpered into the sitting room in an attempt to get away from Ma's ire, but, sensing the benevolence of the mood and realizing that I would most likely escape being in Ma's dog house, I crouched, my head between my fore legs, the stub of my tail firmly lodged between my hind. I was eyeing the evolving scene intently, prepared for recriminations but hopeful of escape.

Once Ma realized that no one minded being cheated of their cheese, her laughter turned from brittle to throaty – a sure indication of sincerity. That was a relief to me, and, giving way to the urge to display how relaxed I was, I turned onto my back and started to roll hither and thither, yapping so evocatively that the nice fat man said, "Your dog is a real character."

"I suppose she is," Ma agreed.

"Dogs should be characters. It means they're happy and well adjusted."

"By and large she is a good girl, though never was anyone more aptly named than Tum Tum," Ma said. "She would eat for twenty five hours a day if she could."

As Ma had put it, the harbingers had turned out to be good, for by the time everyone had left; this glorious intervention of mine had been turned into such an occasion for mirth that she didn't even bother to reprimand me when we were alone

She did, however, ensure that she never again put cheese to breathe within my reach. So, from then until I crossed over into Pet Heaven, I had to endure the torment of smelling the most delicious cheeses wafting downwards from the top of the large refrigerator, which was decidedly out of my reach if still within range of my olfactory sensibilities.

Those cheeses aside, the contents of the refrigerators were not beyond my ken, and on the few occasions that Ma actually left me in the house alone for any length of time, she always returned to find that I had cleaned out everything worth eating.

At first, she was mystified as to how I had engineered the feat. Because the refrigerator doors were magnetized so shut of their own accord, she would come back home to see a kitchen in apparent good order. Then she would open the fridge and lo and behold, where there had once been food there was now a void. The first time, I could tell that she was filled with admiration for my initiative. Her voice was not only laden with respect but she was laughing as she said, "I have to take my hat off to you, Tum Tum. You are truly inventive. How on earth did you manage to swipe all that food?"

The second time, she possessed significantly less humour, and by the third, when I polished off a leg of Parma ham she had brought back from Mallorca, she had run out of patience. "You are incorrigible," she snapped, and promptly linked me up to my leash and marched me to the household department of Peter Jones in

Sloane Square, where she bought child locks for the refrigerator doors. I don't mind telling you, those locks were absolutely dreadful. Two strips of plastic with interlocking hooks meant that the more pressure you put on the door, the tighter the contraption held. But I was not a Springer Spaniel for nothing. It was bad enough that I had to live with those wonderful food scents bombarding my fantastic sense of smell while Ma was around, but really, it was wholly unreasonable to expect a hunter like me, when I was on my own, to politely decline an invitation that was perpetually being issued from behind closed doors. So I did what any other conscionable gun dog would do. As soon as Ma was out the door, my right paw was in the gap between the fridge door and the body of the fridge itself. I scratched and scratched away at the rubber which insulated this most inviting piece of electrical equipment, intent on forcing a breech until I heard Ma return home, at which point I rushed into my basket so that she wouldn't find me out.

Thereafter, I didn't mind it so much when Ma left me alone, for it gave me the opportunity to return to my task. For weeks on end I would intently paw away at the same spot until one afternoon while she was out moving the car, I heard something go pop and saw a piece of white plastic – *the* piece of white plastic which was one half of the child lock – whiz over my head in the direction of the kitchen table.

As all wise people know, and I was about to discover for the first though by no means last time in my life, doggedness does win the day. Having sprung the lock, I sprang the door and without further ado liberated the remnants of a delicious leg of lamb as well as a bowl of gravy and several potatoes which had been roasted in goose fat. I was just starting on a rib of beef which Ma had seasoned and left in a plastic bowl on the top shelf when she returned home and caught me in the act.

She didn't know whether to laugh or cry. "I don't believe it. I don't believe it," she repeated, shaking her head from side to side the way we all do when we're stymied.

"What am I going to do with you? You are incorrigible," she said, using that word again as she bent down to pick up the bowl which had somehow slithered across the floor. "Get into your basket," she growled authoritatively, then started to mutter to herself, wondering how I had managed to get the door open until she happened upon the part of the plastic lock which had flown over my head and landed under the kitchen table.

Seeing that the double-faced adhesive strip which secured the lock to the side of the refrigerator was no longer stuck to the plastic, she wrongly supposed that it had lost its sticking power. Sometimes it is very annoying when people fail to give you the credit that is your due, but this was not one of those occasions. I was supremely relieved when she piped up with, "Ah, the glue's come unstuck," entirely missing my contribution to the enterprise. I knew I was home free when she added, "I suppose one can hardly blame you for availing yourself of the goodies on offer if the door wasn't locked properly," and before I could say, "Silly Mummy," she was attaching the leash to my collar for us to go back to Peter Jones for some more of the double-sided adhesive tape which secured the lock to the refrigerator.

Of course, wise people know why they say that experience teaches wisdom. Now that I knew that the judicious pressing of paw between door and refrigerator could result in the double-sided adhesive losing its tensile strength, making one side of the lock fly across the room after it gave off a delightful popping sound, I almost welcomed being left alone.

Not appreciating that things had changed and I could now be trusted to remain home alone without barking as long as worthwhile scents emanated from the refrigerator, Ma still took me out with her as often as possible. Even though I still enjoyed being out and about, I welcomed the few opportunities that arose for me to remain at home so that I could apply myself to the intoxicating prospect of pawing my way to culinary satisfaction.

Because these occasions were sporadic and never of a long enough duration for me to put sufficiently sustained pressure on the double-sided adhesive, each time I returned to the task of loosening that wretched lock's hold on the refrigerator it was as if I had never done so before. Experience, however, had already taught me that I only needed to keep at it long enough for my labours to bear fruit - meat actually, but one doesn't want to be too pedantic and ruin a well-known metaphor by mixing up the food that I really love with that which I would happily leave behind.

Not being stupid, I appreciated how imperative it was that Ma not find out how I occupied myself when she was out. So I was careful to keep an ear cocked for when she opened the front door. As soon as I heard her key in the lock, I would rush straight to my basket, lay my head on my paw, and pretend to be chilling out. I must have been pretty convincing, for she always greeted me by rustling the hair on my forehead before bending down to kiss me between the eyes.

It took me weeks before I heard the welcome sound of the lock popping for a second time. This time, however, Ma returned home after I had consumed a whole raw chicken and about six varieties of cheese as well as their wrappers. There being nothing else of interest for me to liberate, I took my rather heavy tummy over to my basket and was fast asleep when Ma came into the kitchen. Because the refrigerator door had shut itself under the magnetic force which is a feature of all modern refrigerators, she didn't even realize how enterprising I had been until she went to cook the chicken later that evening.

Poor Ma. I might almost have laughed at how innocent she could sometimes be if I hadn't loved her so much. Once more muttering to herself as she wondered how the door had unsprung itself for a second time; she tried to work out what had happened. Of course, she got it wrong, telling Pa that she was convinced that the double-sided adhesive Peter Jones was selling was no good, and must be giving way as soon as I put the slightest pressure on it. She said she was planning to drive into the City the following morning to buy "proper double-sided adhesive" from a popular ironmonger whose premises were more or less opposite the Tower of London. This, naturally, enabled Ma and Pa to have one of their romantic lunches in the City, with me ensconced on the back ledge of the car watching all those stockbrokers and bankers walk by in their pin-striped suits and brollies, while the fridge door remained maddeningly accessible with no one to benefit from it.

It was only after I had successfully dislodged the child-lock for a third time that I inadvertently provided Ma with the evidence of where my aptitude lay. She came home to find that I had shredded the rubber surrounding the door with my paw. Proud of her Eureka moment, she informed me that we were moving home the following week, and "you can be sure that I'll find a way of securing the refrigerator doors in our new kitchen in such a way that not even you can get into it."

Chapter Four

On Maundy Thursday, 1986, Ma and I moved from the top of Eaton Terrace to the bottom.

Although Eaton Terrace is a relatively short street, and the distance between the two properties can have been no more than a few hundred yards, the improvement was significant insofar as I was concerned.

Firstly, West Eaton Place had no garden, while our new home not only had spacious grounds, but was an apartment on the ground floor of a six storey building that overlooked the busy intersection of Eaton Terrace and Ebury Street.

Our block was one of four matching apartment buildings designed in the Art Deco style after the Second World War and built by the 2nd Duke of Westminster on bombed out land, which was beautifully landscaped, with lush lawns surrounded by peach rose bushes that provided a low border between the grounds and the passersby on Ebury Street. Unlike most London properties, our new flat was suffused with light. The sitting room alone had four large windows and a French door on three of its four sides, as well as generous ledges where Ma placed photographs in silver frames which she broke up with the odd vase of flowers or decorative plate. These ledges were ideal for paws too, the only problem being that I was still not allowed onto the sofas, and had to snatch my moments when Ma wasn't around.

All this was about to change in a wholly unexpected way. A few

Our new flat was a decided improvement, with its own garden which I soon was able to run around without a lead.

weeks after we moved in, Ma's brother asked her to accompany him for the May Day weekend to stay with a friend of his and her two children in the North of England. Something of a cleanliness and orderliness freak who disliked having children and dogs around him, Uncle Mickey suggested that she leave me in kennels. Naturally, Ma refused, and since he really wanted her company, he made the tremendous concession of having me along as well.

On the appointed Friday afternoon, Ma and I duly set off up to Uncle Mickey's flat on Elgin Avenue in Maida Vale, where we were due to link up with him. When we arrived, he was nowhere near ready, which was no surprise to me, for punctuality seemed to be his deadly enemy and I had never witnessed my uncle being on time, not even once, in the many months I had know him.

With his cranky, Victorian-bachelor attitude to children and dogs – the former to be seen and not heard, the latter to be neither seen nor heard – it was no surprise when we arrived at his house to find that he led Ma into the drawing room to listen to a new recording of the pianist Emil Gilels, while I was very firmly locked out.

Ma protested. "She's not bothering anyone. Why can't she stay with us?"

"Let her stay in the passage," he said. "It will be good for her to learn some independence."

Talk about boring. I sat down on my haunches, hoping he would let me in soon, and, when it became obvious that he had no intention of doing so, I went in search of something to do.

Walking down the passage past the guest bedroom into the dining room, I detected one long panorama of antisepsis. Not only was everything spotless, but it smelt that way too. So I sauntered into the kitchen, hopeful that at least there I would find something to make my nose twitch. But not even there was there a scent to appeal to a human, much less a dog. As I sniffed the refrigerator hopefully, I could hardly believe that it was completely lacking in anything tempting. Either it was empty, or everything in it was frozen. So I turned tail and headed into Uncle Mickey's bedroom, where the prospects of entertaining myself with some tasty morsel turned out to be considerable. Under the bed was a pair of spanking new bedroom slippers with leather hand-tooled bottoms of unsurpassable softness. Swooning with pleasure, I pulled one out with my right paw and masticated upon it for a good ten or fifteen minutes. When I felt I had it done sufficient justice, I looked up to see a very interesting item on the bed. I had never seen anything like it before, so I did not yet know that it was a painting by a highly regarded young artist called Everald Something-or-the-Other which Uncle Mickey was planning to get framed. All I knew was that it was something colourful to behold and enticing to smell, the linseed oil being especially attractive. So, even though I wasn't allowed onto beds, I jumped up, pushed it off, and then set to chewing one of its edges from the safety of the floor.

I was so preoccupied with what I was doing that I didn't even notice Uncle Mickey enter the room. There was no mistaking his arrival, however, when he let out the most unholy roar. "Look at what your dog is doing," he shrieked as he yanked the painting out of my mouth.

Ma came flying into the room. "Oh, my God, I am so sorry. Tell me where you got the slippers and I……..

"The slippers don't matter. It's the painting that counts," a clearly upset Uncle Mickey spluttered.

"Of course I must pay the restorers……" Ma started to say, but he cut her off.

"That's not the issue. It's whether they can repair it at all." He was turning the painting over in his hands, looking at it first this way, then that, as if by inspecting it he could somehow reverse the effect my teeth had had upon it.

Now, you would have to be a particularly unconscionable dog not to be embarrassed. I hadn't planned to inflict any damage upon either the slippers or the picture. I had simply been occupying myself, masticating the way all young dogs need to until they are about eighteen months old. So I hung my head to one side and uttered an apology in my very best forgive-me voice.

"Look at that, she's telling you she's sorry," Ma said, ever proud of my accomplishments, even in extenuating circumstances such as these.

Uncle Mickey shot her a look laden with the accompanying scent of annoyance before softening. "She is apologizing," he agreed. "I suppose she didn't know better. Maybe I shouldn't have locked her out without a ball or something like that to play with…."

"She couldn't have got up to mischief if she'd been with us," Ma agreed. "I am so sorry…"

"Let's not make it spoil our weekend," Uncle Mickey said. "Though I will say, you spoil that dog. The way you carry on, anyone would think she was your child."

"But she is. She is," Ma said, voicing a self-evident truth, as Uncle Mickey gave his picture one last lingering look before packing it away out of my reach, which struck me as a classic case of shutting the stable door after the horse has bolted.

A few minutes later Uncle Mickey led us to where his car was parked. While he loaded the luggage into the boot, Ma settled herself in the front passenger seat with me at her feet. From then, until we reached Kirkby Stephen five and a half hours later, the three of us had a companionable and uneventful time. The weekend turned out to be pleasurable too; because the son of the house, Oliver, convinced Ma to let me off my lead and start to train me to walk to heel without anything to constrain me but obedience. Although I have to admit that Ma's interpretation of walking to heel was considerably more flexible than your average dog-handler, in that I was allowed to walk a few feet in front of, behind or beside her, we were both so content with this new arrangement that she felt able to perpetuate it in London.

Arriving back at home late on the Monday evening, she parked in a resident's parking bay opposite the main gate and for the first time ever, let me cross the road without being on the lead. I made it into the garden without any difficulty. This evidently lulled her into an even greater degree of false confidence than she had already possessed, and, after we had stashed our luggage in the flat, she took me for my last-thing-at-night walk around the garden, waxing enthusiastic about how well I was doing. She seemed to have forgotten that I was never kept on my lead in the confines of our garden or the park, so allowing me to do my business without my lead was not ratification of my newly-learnt ability to walk somewhat-to-heel.

The following morning, we both crossed the deserted road without a problem, jumped into the car, and set off for the park, where we always met Pa and Sootie at 6:45 a.m. They had arrived ahead of us and were already out of their car when we pulled into the parking lot at the Royal Albert Hall. As soon as we stopped, Ma opened the driver's door and allowed me to leap out without putting on my lead.

Seeing Sootie and Pa about to cross the road, I set off in their direction. I detected Ma behind me, rushing to close the gap between us. So I increased my pace.

"Tum Tum, wait for me," she called out, as the gap between us was closing. But I could see that the gap between Pa, Sootie and me wasn't, so I started to run.

"Tum Tum, wait for me," Ma ordered. She was now hurtling towards me, which of course only encouraged me to continue in the direction I was heading.

I could see that Pa and Sootie had crossed the road and were now headed into the park. Not only was I keen to join them, but I also wanted them to see what a big, grown up girl I was. I could walk almost-to-heel. So I started across the road just as a car came out of nowhere going well over the speed limit.

I cannot in all honesty say I saw it or was even aware of its existence. Springer Spaniels are notoriously oblivious to traffic, something neither Ma nor I knew, so I was blissfully unaware of what was about to happen as the vehicle slammed into me.

The next thing I knew, I was in the middle of the road with Ma crouching beside me gasping for breath and saying over and over again, "Oh, my God, I don't believe this," while Pa bent down to check that I was alive and Sootie sniffed me to see what she could discern. The driver of the car, who, irony of irony, turned out to be both a working colleague of Pa's as well as an old school friend, had been rushing to make an important breakfast meeting in the City. He was apologizing profusely, swearing he had not seen me, while Ma now started to howl, "We've got to get her to a vet. Oh, my God, she looks as if her back is broken. This can't be happening."

Pa quickly dispensed with his friend and ordered Ma to stay with me. She stood in the middle of the road holding up her hand to warn any other approaching cars that something was amiss. "I'll get the car," Pa said.

"No, I'll get mine," Ma said. "You'll have to lift her. I can't. I'll drive."

"Take Sootie and put her in my car," Pa said. "She'll only be in the way if we take her with us."

While Pa held up his hand to keep the traffic away from us, Ma grabbed Sootie's lead, ran towards Pa's car as if she were being pursued by the furies, shut her in Pa's car, and was back with our own Renault so quickly that she might well have broken a world record for sprinting as well as car racing had it been an official race. She pulled up in the middle of the road, turned on her flashers, jumped out to open the back door for Pa, and gently patted me as he settled me in his lap on the back seat, all the while exuding a lexicon of scents each of which reeked of anxiety and distress.

Although Ma took care not to jolt me, she kept on her flashers as she tore up Kensington Road and down Sloane Street heading for the Elizabeth Street Clinic, which would normally have been about twelve minutes away, but took her no more than five.

"I only hope she's not too badly hurt," she kept on saying, between great heaving sobs, while Pa tried to prepare her for the possibility that my spine might be broken and I would have to be put down.

Ma, however, was not prepared to countenance that possibility, even though she was the one who had first mooted it, and kept on saying, "God won't be so cruel. He won't. He can't."

Although I was now in pain, the shock which had initially caused numbness now given way to unwelcome feeling, I cannot tell you how reassured I was by Ma's attitude. I could tell that she loved me unreservedly and would do anything to save my life, and while I didn't know what was wrong with me either, I did know that I could no longer walk, for when I tried to move, I couldn't.

As soon as we pulled up outside the clinic, Ma ran to open the door for Pa. While he eased himself and me out of the car, Ma tore up the steps and started ringing the doorbell insistently. One of the nurses opened the door, as Pa and I joined her.

Without saying a word, Kathy, who would become a great favourite of mine, shot off to fetch the vet. Sandy was a tall, kindly, handsome Australian whom I had seen once or twice for things like vaccinations. He ran from his flat above the clinic to the examination table, where Pa had gently laid me to rest, asking what had happened. Pa explained and Ma begged him to save my life while he examined me. "We'll have to do an X-Ray, but it doesn't look as if her spine's broken," he said, much to Ma's relief.

Ten minutes later, Sandy was scrubbing up for surgery, having determined that I had a badly broken hip and leg. While there was some doubt that I would ever walk again properly, he was confident that, barring some misadventure, I was likely to live.

With those words, Ma collapsed into Pa's arms, tears of relief pouring onto his track suit. He, however, had to leave to pick up Sootie and his car, so after he had given me a long, lingering kiss on my neck and wished me well, he pecked Ma on the cheek and told her to phone him as soon as I was out of surgery. He knew Ma better than to question whether she would be staying with me.

The joy of having a loving, devoted mother is that she can be relied upon to do the right thing at the right time. Therefore, the last thing I saw and heard prior to the anaesthetic taking hold was Ma telling me how much she loved me and how she was sure I would be fine once Sandy had fixed me up. While she was saying this, she was stroking me tenderly, saying, "I love you, Tum Tum. You must be a big, brave girl and do all in your power to assist Sandy so that you come through this operation with flying colours. You don't need to worry about going to sleep. You'll be fine. Sandy and I are here to take good care of you."

Once I was under, Sandy informed Ma that there was no point in waiting while he performed the surgery. Our flat being a three minute drive away, he advised her to go back home and relax until he telephoned her to tell her what the outcome was.

Three hours later, Sandy telephoned Ma to tell her that the damage to my hip and leg had been considerable. He had had to wire me up. There was every likelihood that I would limp severely, but also that I would be able to walk. He explained that I had a shunt which meant that I would suppurate body fluids as I healed, but this was necessary in the light of the injuries I had sustained. He advised keeping me in the hospital for the next two or three days, but said that she could come and visit whenever she wanted. So Ma walked over five minutes later and sat with me in my cage for an hour, stroking me gently and just letting me know she loved me. Sometimes, I was conscious, sometimes not, but at all times I could sense her love, which was a great balm.

Although Ma returned home for lunch, afterwards she came and sat with me again for about another hour, this time bringing a book to read. Later that afternoon, she was back again with the book, and that evening she came for a good two hours after dinner.

I have to say, I found her visits most uplifting. They helped to pass the time with something approximating normality. Just knowing she was there made things seem better, even though I was woozy from the drugs to combat the pain, and there was no way I could delude myself into thinking that things were good.

At the end of the third day, Sandy allowed Ma to take me home. I still could not walk, so he showed Ma how to use a towel under my belly as a support when I needed to do my business. He warned her, "She can have no weight on her hind quarters until she's healed."

He also taught her how to lift me without injuring me further.

This accident showed Ma in a new light. Until then, she had been insistent that I mustn't go onto her treasured sofas. She had bought them at Harrods in 1977. They were custom-made, covered in an elegant and very expensive ivory and salmon chintz sea-island cotton, and in such good condition that they still looked brand new nearly a decade later. Notwithstanding all of that, as soon as we were home, she put me to rest on one of them, where she had already spread towels underneath a large piece of vet-bed which Sandy had recommended she purchase. By this time, I was intimately acquainted with vet-bed, a man-made fabric that looked like sheepskin but remained dry to the touch even after liquids (urine especially) had been poured onto it. I had been lying on it at the clinic, where it lined the cages we animals were kept in, all 'accidents' being absorbed by the newspaper underneath it.

Ma had a habit of talking to me as if I were capable of understanding what she was saying, which of course I was. I was therefore half expecting an explanation, and sure enough, out she came with one. "Sandy says it's going to be a long time before you're well enough to walk, and it would be too cruel to have you stay on the hard floor where you might develop sores, so you've been promoted to the sofas," she said, bending down to kiss me on my forehead. Normally, I would have been rolling around on my back on the floor at this, and Ma would have been tickling my tum-tum, which sent me into ecstasy, but this was a pleasure which we would both have to forgo until I regained my dexterity.

"You are definitely a good mother, Ma," I yapped. "Thank you so much for allowing me onto the sofas."

"Think nothing of it, Tum Tum. It's the least I can do," she replied. "But you're going to have to sleep on a baby's rubber under-sheet, as I really can't face you ruining the bed-linen as well as the sofas."

A few days later, Ma took me back to the clinic for a check-up. Sandy was pleased with my progress, but on the next visit, he expressed concern that my bones were not knitting as quickly as he would have liked. Adopting a watch and wait posture, he was sufficiently concerned on the next visit to suggest operating again.

This was the start of three months of operations, pins, wiring, suppuration, and dashed hopes. Just when I began to despair that the saga would never end, the bones started to knit and he could safely remove the pins as well as the shunts from which the build-up of fluids oozed, and close the open wounds. During this time, Ma was a true Stoic. You would never have known how much she had loved those sofas, which had been totally ruined. But she didn't care. As long as I was on the mend and comfortable, that was all that mattered to her.

I knew without a doubt that I was on the road to recovery when Ma was visited by Mr Hari the upholsterer. He arrived armed with a tape measure and his clients' notebook. As he set about measuring the sofas to re-cover them in spanking off-white cotton pique which Ma had bought on one of the shopping trips she was still making without me – I had to stay at home the whole time (and never once did I yap out a protest, just in case you are tempted to think I would have taken advantage of the situation!) – I hoped she wouldn't want to revert to that tiresome old practice of keeping me off the sofas once she had taken delivery of his handiwork.

I couldn't be sure; however, when I would be deemed fit enough to stop lolling about on them, for I was still not allowed to put any weight on my hind quarters, not even when doing my business. Ma still had to lift me everywhere, and while I had become adept at slithering off the sofas when I wanted a change of scene, I still couldn't climb back onto them without Ma's assistance.

By the end of the following week, I was feeling well enough to yearn to resume our old habits of being out and about as well as running in the park with Sootie and Pa. I could tell it was only a matter of time before I was able to do so, as it now felt all right to put some weight on my hind legs. Gingerly at first, then with ever-increasing confidence as I became aware that I could do so without pain, I started using my good leg and thigh as often as I needed to. Being three legged was awkward, however, so I soon was also putting weight on my bad leg and hip. Although initially nervous, I followed my instincts and found that they were the ideal gauge for what I could and could not do. Rather sooner than anyone would have expected, I was walking pretty normally, with only the slightest suggestion of a limp.

Ma and Pa were as pleased with my progress as I was, especially when Sandy told them that the time had come for us to resume our runs in the park. "I don't think she'll improve much beyond this," he said. "I'm really pleased with the outcome. I thought she'd have a bad limp. Now she barely limps"

In fact, Sandy was wrong. Before the month was out, I was walking without even a suggestion of a limp. Only when I ran was there a clue of the ordeal I had been through, for I ran at a slight angle rather than straight. But even then, you would have had to be very observant to notice even that, so slight was it. And I could still swim without any difficulty. This was a welcome relief, because, prior to my accident, one of my favourite pastimes had been swimming in the Serpentine with Sootie.

Initially, Ma had been highly dubious of that activity. With her North American background and its attendant emphasis on hygiene, she had not wanted me to go into "that dirty water," as she bluntly put it. But Pa had a laird's disdain for "all that nonsense" and believed that "what's not killing is fattening." When Ma had seen that it was well-nigh impossible to keep me from following Sootie into the

Talking to our beloved housekeeper Mackie at the end of my recovery from the comfort of the sofas.

Serpentine – and that there was no way she could convince Pa that she was being anything but a "silly goose and too metropolitan," she bowed to the inevitable. Which is how Sootie and I came to have an early morning swim four or five mornings a week, rain or shine, sun or snow.

Although you could not have said that Ma was exactly enthusiastic about my swimming before the accident, after it she was positively avid. This is where her American heritage came into play in a most welcome way, for she understood the merits of exercise in a way that few Europeans did in those days when swimming pools were things that existed only south of Bordeaux and gyms and health clubs were so new to our culture that exercise of any sort was reserved for school children in blue shorts and white socks on freezing playing fields. So, on the very first morning Ma took me for a run after Sandy had given me the all-clear, and Sootie led the way into the Serpentine in her usual manner, as I looked around to see if Ma would object to my joining her, I could hardly believe my luck when she said, "Go on, Tum Tum. The exercise will do you good." And that weekend, when Ma and I went to Battersea Park while Pa and Sootie were in Scotland to tend to his shoot, she embarked upon another first: She actually encouraged me to swim in

Running in the garden with enthusiasm albeit at a slight angle.

the lake there, instead of calling to me insistently the way she had always done previously did when I used to skirt close to it in the hope that I could slip in without her noticing.

Life was certainly looking up in unexpected ways. But I resumed our former activities with one substantial difference. By virtue of still being allowed onto the sofas, I now had access to the window ledges, where I could rest my front paws as I looked at the world passing by on Ebury Street. Although the accident had been awful, the aftermath proved the truth of the maxim that "out of evil cometh forth good". My horizons had expanded in ways that would never have been possible beforehand. Now, I had passing parades whether I was out and about on the window-ledge of the car or at home with Ma. Life had certainly looked up in a wholly unexpected way.

Chapter Five

It's great to be young and healthy, with not a care in the world except how to open the refrigerator door. I freely admit it: Once I recovered from my accident, I had a wonderful life. It was both regular and varied. I cannot really say I had one complaint or wanted anything to be different, except of course for the removal of the new and more effective locks which Ma had got for the refrigerator. They were impervious to the pressure of my paws, but this was a minor detail, for I was practically never at home alone any more.

But my life was about to change in a major and permanent way.

In February 1987, Ma and I were walking on Cliveden Place towards Sloane Square, when we saw a taxi do a U-turn. It pulled up just in front of us, by the pedestrian crossing where the David Mellor shop was. Its occupant, a young woman with long, thick and wavy brown hair, jumped out. "You might think that this is crazy," she said with charming urgency, "but I couldn't help noticing your dog. It's so beautiful I couldn't resist stopping. Do you mind if I pat it?"

Now, Ma might be adventurous and a fully-paid-up member of the canine-love-club, but even she has her limits. Just the way she said: "Not at all," I knew she harboured deep reservations about the turn events had taken.

This stranger bent down and started to stroke me so gently and lovingly that I warmed to her immediately. I therefore gave her a huge wet kiss right across her nose. This made her gurgle delightedly, which naturally resulted in me hunkering down for some really serious kissing. As I did so, I knocked her over onto the pavement. She started to laugh and laugh and laugh, while I set about the serious business of showing her how loving I truly was.

"Stop that right this instant," Ma ordered, yanking my lead to no effect whatsoever, as she apologized to the strange lady I had pinned down beneath me. She continued gurgling with delight as I provided her with a genuine love-fest the like of which she might never have had before. Until Ma grabbed my collar and pulled me off.

I could tell, however, that this nice stranger wanted more love, so once she was back on her feet, I sprang up onto her bosom and yapped out my desire to give her even more licks and kisses.

"I cannot think what has got into her. Tum Tum, stop that immediately," Ma commanded as she apologized yet again. It took a few more minutes before sufficient order was restored for Ma and this lovely lady to introduce themselves to one another. While they did so, Nicky caressed my neck. Then, and only then, did she make the purpose of her stop apparent.

"I hope you won't think me crazy, but I have never seen a more splendid Springer Spaniel. My brother is getting married in summer and I wanted to give my sister-in-law-to-be, who adores springers, a puppy. And she and my boy Timothy would have the most beautiful puppies."

"She's only a year and a half. I hadn't planned to breed from her until she's five," Ma said dubiously.

"Before you say no, can I introduce you to Timothy? He's a ravishingly handsome boy and I know they'll have the most marvellous puppies. If not in time for Charlie's wedding, then later."

Nicky and Ma then swapped telephone numbers, and sure enough, when she brought Timothy around a few days later, both Ma and I took to him in a big way. He really was ideal husband-material. Beautiful, well-proportioned, good-natured, black and white and affectionate, with a fine pedigree. In short, he was the embodiment of masculine Springer Spaniel perfection.

I could tell Ma was losing the battle to preserve my status as a maiden when Pa arrived, fell under Timothy's spell, and declared, "They'd have the most magnificent puppies. You should go for it. Tum Tum might be young, but she's not too young to start breeding. In fact, there's a school of thought which thinks that she's the ideal age for her first litter."

Although Ma remained reluctant to inflict maternity upon me until I was more mature, she nevertheless yielded to Pa and Nicky's blandishments when Pa pointed out that I would at least have the companionship of another dog if she kept one of my litter. Which is how I came to be married, with three separate receptions on the 15th, 16th, and 17th March 1987.

There is no doubt. I was no blushing bride. Young though I was, I was eager for matrimony. I had had seasons before, and was at the receptive stage of my cycle when Nicky brought Timothy round to our flat for the wedding ceremony. But a girl needs a bit of courting even when she is keen to walk up the aisle. So, when Timothy roared into the sitting room with tail wagging and masculinity oozing from every pore, and we had dispensed with the necessary sniffs which all dogs indulge in when greeting each other, I stood still and allowed him to lick my neck with a graciousness that seemed to surprise Ma. She laughed and said to Nicky, "Look at this. Tum Tum is such a coquette. She's making him work for her consent."

Undeniably, Timothy's tongue was pouring magic upon my neck. I felt myself swoon with pleasure, and, shortly after that, I decided that I would definitely accept him as my husband when the time came for us to exchange our vows.

From then onwards, events escalated rapidly. One moment Timothy and I were two separate entities who each had four paws on the ground, and the next, we were one body, with only six paws on the ground; his fore legs were wrapped nicely around me in a delectable hug. The strain on my back was not particularly pleasant, however, so I tried to wriggle into a more comfortable position. In doing so, I nearly toppled both Timothy and myself over, and succeeded in sending one of Ma's mahogany side tables flying across the room. As it did so, Nicky jumped up, grabbed both of my new husband's front legs, and gently steered them off me in such a way that he and I were each able to stand, back to back, eight paws firmly on the floor, though we remained joined as man and wife.

"How do we separate them?" Ma said, an element of panic in her voice. I could tell she had visions of Timothy and me being permanently stuck together, which just went to show that she was as much a novice at this mating business as Timothy and I were.

Nicky, however, was more experienced in these matters, so she set about reassuring Ma. "We don't separate them. They will be locked together for a few minutes. It's nature's way of maximizing the chances of conception. If we tried to separate them, Tum Tum's insides might be damaged. When they're ready, she'll release him naturally."

Nicky then stroked both of us and brought up the question of whether Ma would allow us to have more than one reception that afternoon. "I don't want them to overdo things," Ma said. "I'd prefer it if we stagger things over three days. That way we increase the odds of her getting pregnant without running the risk of his hurting her."

Of course, there was no guarantee that I would become pregnant, not even after three separate wedding receptions on three consecutive days. But I definitely was, as Ma discovered within weeks, when she took me to see Simon, the new vet at the Elizabeth Street Clinic who took over from Sandy when he went back to Australia.

From then until I went into labour, Ma insisted on educating herself about the process of whelping, as having puppies is known in veterinary circles. She had not had babies of her own, so she got Simon to give her a tape, which she looked at time and again until all its information was fixed in her mind. Then, and only then, did she give it back to Simon.

Ma was not the sort of person who worried needlessly, but she did believe in being what she called "sensible", so, as I got larger and larger, she checked with Simon to see if it was all right for me to continue going for runs and swims in the park. I suspect she was almost as pleased as I was to discover that the answer to both questions was yes. I was young, fit and healthy, and pregnancy was a natural process so there was no need to curtail any of my activities, none of them being dangerous or excessively strenuous.

Because my due date could have been sixty three days after any one of the three occasions upon which Timothy and I had celebrated our marriage, Ma started to become anxious as the first of those possible dates approached. Bright and early on the morning of the 16th May, 1987, we therefore walked round to the Elizabeth Street Clinic for her to borrow the whelping tape again. As she and I lay on our bed watching the dogs going into various stages of labour, then giving birth to puppies, I could sense her anxiety. I therefore snuggled up close to her, more to reassure her than myself. While I was now very large indeed, and was actually starting to become uncomfortable enough to have refused to run that morning – though I did amble - I was nevertheless feeling well enough to have no fear. But I did notice Ma watching me like a hawk all that day. And during the night, I slept more soundly than she did, for on several different occasions I was vaguely aware of her checking to see that I was still all right.

During the day of the 17th May, I chilled out, too laden to do anything but eat, take short walks, and rest. All those babies in my tummy were definitely starting to become restive as well as uncomfortable. The desire to expel them was increasing by the moment, then suddenly, while Ma and Pa were having a quiet supper, there were really severe rumblings in my tummy and my breathing pattern changed. I started to pant and pant and pant, but for some reason I wasn't unnerved by this new experience. It was so natural that I found myself just going with the flow. Then, as suddenly as the rumbling and panting had started, they stopped.

This was both a relief and a problem, for I could sense that the only way I was going to get those puppies out of my tum tum was to push them out. One virtue of being a dog is that we don't fight against natural situations the way human beings often do, so instead of trying to force a solution, I lay back in the whelping basket Ma had bought for me, and relaxed.

I don't know how long it was before I was hit by a second wave of rumblings and quickened breathing, but this time I sat up in my basket and started to pant even more strongly than before as I felt my tum tum constrict. "She's in labour," Pa said.

"Yes. I can recognize that from the whelping tape," Ma agreed.

Pa had a business meeting early the following morning, so after he left us relatively early, Ma changed into what she called her "whelping clothes" – a well-used track suit that she would otherwise have thrown out. She then moved my whelping basket into our bedroom, placing it right beside the bed so that she could look down at what was happening without having to crane her neck. Having done that, she said, "I tell you what, Tum Tum. You make yourself comfortable in your whelping basket until you're ready to deliver the puppies. I'll stay up with you. Shall we watch *Marie Antoinette* starring Moira Shearer and Tyrone Power? Aunt Leslie (an American film buff friend of Ma's who loved me) says it has the most beautiful costumes, which I suppose it would have done, as her husband was David Selznick, the head of the studio when the movie was made. I only hope they didn't take too many liberties with the story. Some of those Hollywood histories have such a loose connection with reality that you might as well be watching a work of declarative fiction."

Duly edified, I lay back and enjoyed the relative comfort of regular breathing while Ma reclined on the bed, her right hand dangling so that she could tickle me from time to time. I would have dearly loved to climb into our bed, but I instinctively knew that Ma wouldn't want me popping out puppies on her clean sheets, so after awhile I got up and once more rearranged the newspaper she had laid in the whelping basket, trying to improve upon my efforts earlier in the evening. While I was shredding them with my paws and pushing them into a new and more agreeable arrangement, I felt another wave of short breaths coming on. Before Ma had even finished saying, "Clever girl. You're nesting again just the way they said you would on the tape," I was panting for all my life was worth. This time the rumblings and respiratory changes lasted for even longer than before, and while they were going on my tummy contracted in a way it had not done before. This was a decidedly disagreeable sensation, and I must have given Ma a particularly plaintive look, for she got out of the bed and knelt beside me, stroking me gently while telling me that I had to be a big, brave girl, and "we'll get through this together".

I can vouch for the fact that childbirth is definitely not for wimps. I endured several more hours of ever-lengthening periods of contractions and irregular breathing followed by ever-shorter respites, until Ma started to get worried and telephoned the Elizabeth Street Clinic to speak to the night vet. She advised Ma to drive me around for an examination if no puppies had come within an hour, but just before dawn, as I lay super-panting in my basket with Ma looking down at me from her semi-recumbent posture (she was on her fourth movie of the night), I felt a tremendous contraction followed by a burst of activity and relief as my first puppy popped out.

I didn't even have time to sniff and lick the puppy before Ma had jumped out of bed and was kneeling beside me, gently removing the cowl with her fingers to allow the puppy to breathe the way she had learnt from the whelping tape. I sniffed the puppy as she did so, intent on chewing off the umbilical chord, but she had been warned that I might cause a hernia tearing it off with my mouth, so she squeezed the chord between thumb and index finger until it separated. Then she turned the puppy over to me for me to continue bonding with it by sniffing it, eating its cowl, and, when the placenta came out shortly afterwards, consuming that as well.

Nothing beats experience, that's for sure. Ma was a lot less nervous once she knew that we could cope with the other births without anything going wrong. Simon had told Ma that he thought I was having about five or six puppies. He had also warned her that there might be fairly long gaps between the births. Although she stayed awake for the second and third births, she nodded off around nine o'clock that morning for a good forty five minutes. When she awoke, she was both surprised and pleased to see that I had delivered a fourth puppy without any assistance, and that a fifth was on its way out.

"My goodness, Tum Tum, you've done it. All on your own. You clever girl," Ma said. I could tell by her tone of voice and scent that she was now pretty relaxed, but even so, she stayed up just in case I produced a sixth puppy.

Would you believe it, within five minutes of number six arriving, out slithered a seventh? This was a small but beautiful liver and white boy, and as I was cleaning him up Ma said, "This must be the final one. Simon did say that one or two might be hidden behind their siblings, but I can't believe that *three* would be."

I sincerely hoped Ma was right. I was now completely exhausted. Yet I was also exhilarated. From the moment I suckled my firstborn, I realized I was born to be a mother. I felt an overwhelming surge of love and protectiveness for this new being such as I had never known before. This knowledge was reinforced with each new arrival, whom I would direct onto my breast as soon as I had cleaned it up and consumed its placenta. I cannot tell you how completely I was possessed of a deep feeling of satisfaction as I embraced the role of providing succour that nature had intended for me. I would gladly have suckled twenty puppies.

The next few weeks passed in a dreamlike haze. This was as close to heaven as life on earth could be. Not only was I floating on a cloud

No mother was ever more overjoyed with her babies than I, seen here a few days after their birth.

of deep maternal fulfilment, but Ma, who wanted to be close at hand in case we needed her for anything, stayed in far more than she normally did. On only two or three occasions did she go out for more than an hour or two. As for me, I only ever went outside for walkies or my morning run, which I resumed a week after the puppies arrived. Otherwise, I stayed quietly in the kitchen, in or near the whelping basket, soaking up the joy that being the nursing mother of seven brought.

I had grown in ways I could never have imagined. It was as if my heart had been inflated by all this love I felt and received. And there was the additional and totally unexpected benefit of being allowed to consume all the food I could. Simon at the Elizabeth Street Clinic had told Ma that nursing bitches must not have their diets restricted. They are supposed to feed on demand, with the result that Ma allowed me to eat as much as I wanted. For the first time in my life, I experienced the delicious sensation of satiety followed by yet more satiety as soon as I ate more food. Several times a day, every day, in fact, I would eat and eat and eat while Ma stood over me, her face the very picture of admiration as she repeated, "You must be in pig heaven, Tum Tum. Never have I known any living creature to pack away so much food. Yet you haven't gained a pound since the puppies were born. Simon has to be right. All that food must convert into milk for the puppies. And the puppies are flourishing, though I can't say the same for my back, which feels as if the vertebrae are going to crack under the pressure of the amount of tinned dog food I have to drag home from Safeway for you."

I had produced seven beauties: five boys (two liver and white, three black and white) and two girls, only one of whom was black and white. This was shaping up to be something of a... I won't say problem exactly...more of an issue. Ma had always been adamant that she wanted only a black and white bitch. It had never occurred to her that she would not have an array of black and white puppies to choose from, but nature had conspired with the forces of love and wisdom to deprive her of a choice. Which is how Popsie Miranda came to be foisted upon Ma, for Ma either had to take her or have a liver and white puppy.

At least Ma and Nicky didn't compound the difficulty of restricted choice with a problem that the parents-in-law of many newborn puppies encountered. The convention with litters has always been that the sire's human parents have what they quaintly call "the pick of the litter". This leaves the dam's human parents with second choice. You can imagine how tensions run high when both sets of parents want the same puppy, as often happens. Fortunately for Ma and me, this was not the case with her and Nicky, for Nicky had only ever wanted a black and white dog, while Ma's interest was restricted to the black and white female of the species.

Herein lay the rub, for once the puppies started to develop and display their own personalities, Popsie Miranda proved to be the most timid of the whole litter. While her liver and white sister showed every sign of being as adventurous as her male siblings, joining them in exploring the environs of the kitchen once they gained their earth legs and realized that there was a world beyond the perimeter of the whelping basket, this sole black and white bitch was growing into such a gentle, sensitive little girl that she seemed content to stay in the basket,

or at the very least, near to me when I was out of it. I could tell that Ma was disappointed, and would gladly have swapped Popsie Miranda with her liver and white sister had she been the colour Ma wanted. But, because she wasn't, Ma was faced with what she called "Hobson's choice".

My heart went out to Popsie Miranda. I knew that she was sweetness personified. But I also knew that Ma, who was intent on instilling a greater sense of adventure in

Popsie Miranda was fortunately the only black and white female in the litter.

my little daughter, was not going to give up without making every effort. She went hell for leather to bring out the one quality Popsie Miranda would always lack. On five separate occasions she lifted her out of the basket when Popsie Miranda was nestling close to me, saying, "Come, darling. Join your brothers and sister. There's a whole new world out there, just waiting for you to explore. You'll never find out how wonderful it is if you don't go out and meet it." She then took Popsie to where the others were, but rather than stay with them, Popsie would take one look, turn tail and flee back to me.

Ma didn't like this one bit. "For goodness sake," she would say impatiently, "you're got to get some spirit," her voice and face the embodiment of crestfallen. I could tell that she would gladly have traded Popsie for any of the other puppies, but luck was on all our sides.

Before this became apparent, however, I had to go through the palaver of weaning the puppies. Nature is certainly clever. It encourages even a mother as devoted as I was to release her puppies into adulthood by making them grow teeth which are like shards of glass in one's soft breast tissue. Within days, the once supremely satisfying act of suckling one's puppies becomes so painful that one soon flees at the sight of them.

Fortunately, Ma had learnt her whelping lessons well. At the first sign of this new development, she went out and bought cases of puppy food. Now she had something else to complain about, for the quantities involved were similar to the amount she had had to buy for me while I was breast feeding them.

I also had something to complain about, for no sooner did I wean the puppies, than Ma put me back on the old, healthy diet of two square meals a day instead of the bliss of feeding-on-demand.

Mackie, our housekeeper, also joined the choir of complainers, for once I stopped breast-feeding the puppies, I also stopped cleaning up after them. For Mackie and Ma, this was a downside to puppies which neither of them had thought of as long as I was breast-feeding them and obeying nature's impulse to eat all their droppings, the way all other nursing bitches do. (It is not only a natural practice but also healthy, as Simon had told a horrified Ma when she first telephoned him in a flap to query what had "gone wrong" with me.)

Compounding the problem of the mess the puppies was making was the fact that they were still too young to be let out. They had not yet had their full series of vaccinations and would therefore have been in danger of catching parvo or distemper or any of the other potentially fatal viruses that lurk wherever other animals have trodden, so Ma had no choice but to turn the kitchen and its adjoining balcony into what she now called "the pooh factory".

Although it was obvious that neither Ma nor Mackie relished this new state of affairs, I admired the way they took it in their stride once they accepted its inevitability. They were very British stiff-upper-lip – their noses held firmly in the air, stoically rising above any distaste they would ordinarily have felt for such a mess, and maintaining their good cheer as and when they had to enter the kitchen, whose door now remained firmly shut at all times, all cooking having come to an end until the puppies were able to do their business outside in the garden, or had gone to new homes; whichever was the sooner.

Because Pa did not believe in puppies being given away at the conventional age of eight weeks old, and Ma felt that seven weeks was too young, she now made a concerted effort to divest herself of the puppies she was not planning to keep. This was as much to escape from the mess as anything else. Knowing how she felt, I was not surprised when a variety of adults, some of whom I had never seen before, others of whom were known to me only casually, started coming to inspect the puppies. The way Ma interviewed them, it was obvious that she was determined to allow them the chance to acquire a puppy only if she was satisfied that they would provide her "grandchildren" (as she called the puppies who were going to be given way) a good home.

Each session was rather elaborate. She would take the potential parents into the sitting room and interview them with all the intensity of a spy-mistress at Bletchley Park selecting freedom fighters during the Second World War. One or two lots didn't even make it into the kitchen. Those who did would then be brought into the kitchen to look at the puppies and make a choice. After they had done so, she would take them back into the sitting room with the puppy and me. While they were cooing over the prospective addition to their family,

Ma would be giving them the beady eye – checking to see that they were sufficiently gentle and loving. One prospective parent she allowed to scoop up the puppy and make off with it onto the balcony for an initial exercise in bonding, though I couldn't help but notice that she kept her eyes firmly open to what was happening. Another prospective lot of parents was a journalist with a pretty wife and three lovely children who all loved puppies. They chose Popsie Miranda's mirror image and even named him Timmy, whether in honour of his father or not I never found out, as every time I asked Ma to enquire, she yapped back silly stuff to me without once comprehending what I was trying to ascertain. Another of her friends who ended up with one of the puppies was a social columnist whose daughter fell in love with my second born son, a spirited liver and white beauty whom he ill-advisedly allowed to walk without a lead on the streets of London. This ended in tragedy, for Charley was run down by a car outside Peter Jones when he was only seventeen months old. Ma never held the accident against his Pa or the driver, though she was decidedly upset, even more

Charley and Popsie Miranda in one of the baskets they demolished the day of his departure.

so than I, for dogs have a far more accepting attitude to separation than humans, not only because we are compelled by circumstances to deal with separations which are forced upon us by our human masters, but also because we understand on a fundamental level that earthly separations are short in eternal terms, and that sooner or later, we all catch up with our loved ones in the next life.

This is exactly what has happened with Charley and me. When I arrived in Pet Heaven, he was waiting to greet me, acting for all the world as if the intervening twelve years had been the blink of an eye lid. We picked up right where we had left off, our love for each other as strong as if time and circumstance had never come between us. We are often together now, as close as any loving mother and son can be, and I can truthfully say I enjoy him as much as I do Popsie Miranda, who spent her whole life with me and whom I love to distraction.

How, you may ask, did I cope with saying goodbye to Charley and Timmy and my four other babies when the time came to hand them over to their new parents? As I just said, dogs have a greater serenity about separation than humans do. But that does not mean that we are exactly overjoyed when we see someone coming to take away our little bundles of joy. Of course we feel sad. Of course we would prefer that it were otherwise. But we understand that life on this earth is not an ideal proposition. There is much that all of us have to accept that we would much rather not have to. But canines don't fight against their fate. We accept what we cannot change, turning our spirit to the light and remaining open to joy from whatever source it comes, for that is the only way to keep one's self and one's soul open to all the goodness that exists, and which we can only receive if we keep our hearts in a state of genuine grace.

That is not to say that the days after I lost my six puppies did not present me with the challenge of wading through dampened spirits, for it did. Aside from my own feelings of loss, I could sense Ma's disappointment in Popsie Miranda, which hardly brightened the scenario. But I have never been one to worry needlessly, and I felt sure that once Ma had got used to this new addition to our family, she too would come to love her as much as I did. Which, within weeks, turned out to be the case.

Ma had trained me and now it was my turn to train Popsie Miranda.

I could actually tell that Ma was falling in love with Popsie Miranda before Ma was even aware of that fact. The way her pores started to open up with the scent of love was a complete giveaway. She took to picking up Popsie Miranda and nuzzling her neck with her nose. She would stroke her tummy, which Popsie loved. And Popsie was the most loving individual you could ever imagine. While she had been timid when she sensed that Ma was not so keen on her, once she felt the atmosphere warming up, she could not contain herself: She followed Ma everywhere, playfully yapping at her heels, nestling close to her ankles when she was sitting down, and generally doing all the things a loving dog does to make his or her master or mistress love her. Within a month, Popsie Miranda had so won over Ma with her gentle qualities that Ma said, for the first of many times, "Popsie Miranda, you really are a very good girl, aren't you? So sweet and loving. Just like a ball of love."

One morning, Popsie Miranda looked at Ma. She opened her mouth, drew back her lips and exposed her teeth. Smiling dogs are a rarity at the best of times, with the result that most people do not even know that the capacity exists. Ma was no exception, but, being more

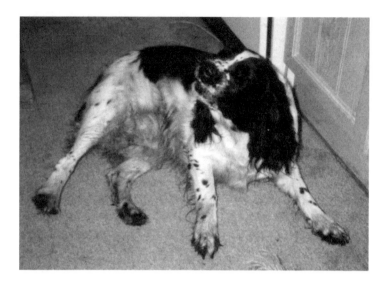

Popsie Miranda's smile was a lot better than Ma's photography, I can assure you.

dogged than the average *homo sapiens*, some atavistic source of animal wisdom was lurking beneath her human instincts. This, coupled with her knowledge of Popsie's character, led her to ask, "Are you skinning your teeth at me or are you trying to smile?" Popsie Miranda then flashed even more teeth, all the while wagging her tail. "You *are* smiling, aren't you?" Ma enthused as Popsie Miranda sidled up to Ma's leg and rubbed herself against it.

"I've never heard of a smiling dog before," Ma said. "But I would stake my life on the fact that you're smiling. Or am I going loopy with love? I'd better ring Simon and ask him before I delude myself into thinking A when I should be thinking B."

With that, Ma marched into her bedroom to ring up Simon. He informed her that it was indeed possible for dogs to smile, though it was such a rarity that it was almost a unique gift.

While Ma was replacing the receiver, she was doing a little jig of joy. "Tum Tum, you have given me the greatest gift any babacita could give a mamacita. Popsie Miranda is not only the most adorable babacita, but she actually *smiles*. Oh, the joy of it all," she said as Popsie Miranda smiled and smiled and smiled and I yapped and yapped and yapped.

Aside from smiling, Popsie Miranda soon displayed another marked characteristic which set her apart from me. Morning, noon or night, she would have one of her soft toys in her mouth. From time to time, she would get up from wherever she was, cross over to Ma, and offer it to her. Ma would take it, thanking Popsie for sharing her treasure with her. Popsie Miranda would make off, find another soft toy, return with it, and either drop it for Ma, retrieving the one she had just given her, or keep it safe and sound in her mouth until she was ready to part with it. She was seldom without something soft and treasured between her jaws, which used to amuse Ma no end. "Popsie Miranda, if you were human you would be a chain-smoker," Ma used to laugh.

Sometimes, Popsie would smile so broadly that the toy would drop out of her mouth, though often as not she managed to execute the double act of an obvious smile while retaining the treasure in her favourite place.

Despite this proclivity, Popsie Miranda was not greedy. Unlike me, she was perfectly happy to eat what was provided for her without wanting more. I envied her such innate satiety, for I was one of those greedy-guts whose tum tum never sent out the message, "Enough is enough."

As Popsie Miranda grew up, Ma started a refrain that would continue for the whole of her life. "Popsie Miranda, you are such a

Popsie Miranda and some of the treasures she used to lug around with her.

good girl that I never have to reprimand you. In fact, there's never ever anything to say to you except how good you are. Unlike Tum Tum and just about everyone else on earth, whom one constantly has to keep in line with judicious applications of encouragement or discipline or whatever, I never have to tell you to walk to heel; or call you to come to me, for you are always where you ought to be. I never have to tell you what you should be doing, as you always somehow do exactly what you should be doing when you should be doing it. If I never told you how good you are, I'd never speak to you. When I stop to think that I would have swapped you for any of the other puppies, it just goes to show how limited my judgement is. You are a true blessing, Popsie Miranda, and I want you to know it."

You can imagine how pleased I was every time Ma poured out this little homily, which she did with regularity over the years. Not only did she appreciate how wonderful Popsie Miranda was, but she was expressing in the English language the very sentiments I could only express in dog-talk. Popsie was that rare individual: the perfect companion. It was as if God had created her with heightened antennae so that she always did exactly what she should have been doing when she should have been doing it, or in the reverse, never doing what she shouldn't be doing.

This knack filled me with admiration, especially as how it was a quality I decidedly lacked. Where she was all sensitivity and delicacy, I roared in with heart open and tail wagging. Where I was noisy – always yapping, as my Aunt Kari would put it, not without an element of affectionate disapproval, while Ma found my "conversational skills", as she called them, amusing and heart warming – she was perennially quiet.

Yet Popsie Miranda was no doormat. She possessed a quiet self-possession that I have seldom seen in another animal, though I have from time to time seen it in great and kind-hearted human beauties. The result was that while she was somewhat reserved with all but the few people whom she liked, she, Ma and I quickly grew into a strong triumvirate. We loved each other passionately and devotedly. We shared trust and took such pleasure in each other's company that many of our happiest moments were when we three were alone together. As long as the three of us were together, life was good and rich.

And, on the occasions when Ma left Popsie Miranda and me to our own devices – usually on the back ledge of the car, while she was out and about – life was twice as good as it had been when I had enjoyed these pursuits on my own, for now I had the perfect companionship of my perfect daughter to add to the delight of watching the world go by.

Chapter Six

It's funny how life divides up into distinct periods even though we might not realize it at the time. With hindsight, I can see that the five years following Popsie Miranda's birth formed what in many ways would be our halcyon days. Ma, Popsie Miranda and I were the inner sanctum, while Pa and Sootie added a pleasurable fourth and fifth dimension. Each morning the five of us went running in Hyde Park.

After Pa and Sootie had left to go back to their house, we would often talk to a nice old lady in a wheelchair with a sweet little lap dog and a companion from the Far East. She loved dogs and always made a big fuss of us, so of course we would give her all the love she needed. I would put my paws on her lap and cover her hands and face with kisses while she chuckled gleefully.

It was only later, when this old lady died and a photograph of her was published in the newspapers, that Ma realized that the raddled but nice old lady was the famous Hollywood movie queen Ava Gardner, who wasn't even so old, though she looked as if she had been around when Moses was crossing the Red Sea. Needless to say, dogs couldn't care less whether people are old or ugly, young or pretty, movie stars or nonentities. As long as they are nice, that's all that matters to us, which, if you ask me, is a far better way to choose your friends than using fame and position as yardsticks for desirability.

On the mornings when this unrecognizable star of the silver screen wasn't around, the three of us would amble back – Popsie and I always safely tethered to our leads - to Ma's car, which fortunately had leather seats, for often as not Popsie Miranda and I were still soaking wet from our swim in the Serpentine. I shudder to think how someone as fastidious as Ma would have coped with us wetting up her car seat morning after morning if it had been cloth.

I always took pride of place beside Ma in the passenger seat, with Popsie Miranda by the window.

Once we were back home, Ma fed us while drawing her bath, after which she invariably took us for a spin around the garden in case we wanted to do anything new. We seldom did, so after sniffing the rose bushes and hoping that MacDonald the porter (a too-efficient Scotsman) had missed bits of food which passersby had thrown into the garden overnight – it is astonishing how disrespectful some people could be of the well-tended gardens (thank God) – we would gobble the morsel or savour the scent before Ma made us go back inside so that she could "begin her day", as she used to put it.

Popsie Miranda and I would lie in the passage and chill while Ma had her bath. After she had addressed the serious business of putting on her make-up, she would haul on some old clothes, comb and spray her hair – a scent we did NOT like – before the three of us adjourned to her writing table in the dining room. I always lay behind her chair on the Persian rug, as had been my wont ever since we had moved from West Eaton Place, and Popsie Miranda,

Hunkering down for the serious business of relaxation with Popsie Miranda.

respecting that, had carved out her own special place. She would crawl under Ma's writing table and nestle directly in front of Ma's feet. Whenever Ma had on sandals, she would give Ma's toes the occasional lick, which always evoked cascades of laughter, though she also always made Popsie Miranda stop before too long, as she found it impossible to concentrate on her work while her toes were receiving my beautiful daughter's ministrations.

It's amazing to look back on the trajectory of Popsie Miranda and Ma's relationship and see how utterly my canine daughter overturned each and every one of my human mother's reservations. Within the space of a few months, you would never have known the rocky start they had had. Popsie Miranda was as close to Ma as it was possible for one soul to be to another. This gave me no end of pleasure. Confident in Ma's love for me, it never once occurred to me to be jealous. On the contrary, I was delighted that the two beings I loved most in the world loved each other as completely as I loved them both. Love, I could see, was not like food. It did not need to be apportioned or rationed. The more there was, the more there was to go around. One didn't need to be greedy or selfish. The more I gave them would be the more I too would have - as long as we all gave and received unselfishly. Which, I am pleased to say, the three of us did.

Pa and Sootie were also unselfish with their love. Though we seldom saw Sootie in the evening, we frequently saw Pa, but they were very much addenda to the triumvirate that Ma, Popsie and I evolved into being.

Between 1987 and 1992 this loving scenario unfolded with nary a glitch. Pa had a shoot in Scotland and occasionally we would join him and Sootie for the weekend, but this was definitely an exception rather than the rule, for Ma was a true metropolitan babe for whom the glories of trudging through soggy fields and woodland 'beating' had no appeal, while lunch at San Lorenzo on a Saturday or a foray through Portobello market was another story entirely.

Not that Ma actually disliked the country. What she disliked was having to stay in a house full of people whom she did not know well. She preferred the peace and quiet of London on the weekends to the hurly burly of your average country house party, where an array of guests more akin to a gaggle of geese than a unit of harmony would gather for the serious business of having what they thought of as fun but she regarded as hard work. Although not shy, Ma had an aversion to "jumping through hoops" as she called the modes of behaviour which

I particularly enjoyed weekends at Sledmere with our hostess, seen here conversing with me.

passed for humans enjoying themselves on country house weekends.

Funnily enough, the one thing which did not make invitations to these weekends wither up was our existence. The English being a nation of dog lovers, most owners of country houses had dogs and they never seemed to mind when their friends brought along their pets as well. Of course, Popsie Miranda and I were both very well trained. We never sat on sofas without being asked to (except at home, of course). We always did our business when and where we should, with the one exception of when we were ushered directly from the car into Ayton Castle. As we had had to endure a long trip from London on the train, followed by a car journey from Berwick-upon-Tweed train station to the castle, with not even a moment for relief, it was wholly unreasonable of them to expect us to wait another hour or two, and after fifty minutes of holding it in, Popsie Miranda could take no more of the waiting and started to yap that she had to go outside. But no one was paying any attention, and, after looking at me plaintively as if to say, "Do you think I will be disgracing you and Ma if I give them one of my solid poohs?" I could not, in all conscience, do anything but yap to her that she should not be embarrassed about relieving herself in these most extenuating of circumstances. Which is precisely what she did. Although David, the laird, teased Ma about us not being house-trained, his wife Christine was having none of it, and quite rightly said that when things like this happen, it's the humans who are at fault, not the dogs.

Popsie Miranda and I enjoyed going on country house weekends like the ones we did to Ayton or to Sledmere, where our host Tatton had a delightful Staffordshire bull terrier who was as humanized as we were – and treated equally well. But by far the stays we loved best were the ones we had with John, who ran a doggie hotel outside London which Ma used to book us into when she went away. I know from some of the friends we made there that their first visits were somewhat fraught, for their human parents had left them there without making a proper introduction first, with the result that they wondered if they had been abandoned. But this is not a mistake Ma made. The day before our first stay at John's, she took us to visit him. The four of us spent a good half an hour touring the place, after which he and Ma had a cup of tea while Popsie Miranda and I made ourselves comfortable on the floor between them. Then she took us back home, where we spent the night as if nothing untoward was going to happen. And indeed nothing untoward did, for by the time she took us back the following day, we were sufficiently familiar with John and his hotel to feel no fear.

Once Ma left us, Popsie Miranda and I could see that John was what the English call a 'good egg'. He had indicated the day before that he allowed all his houseguests the run of his house, but of course humans often say one thing to each other then do quite another to dogs. We soon learnt, however, that this relaxed regimen was no empty promise. Not only did we have unrestricted access to the sofas, but we could also come and go between the house and the back garden via the conservatory as and when we pleased during the day. I cannot tell you what heaven it was to run around the well-fenced garden at the back of his house, where his idea of a dog run was a good acre of lawn bordered by hardy bushes like hydrangeas and rhododendrons. Never before had Popsie Miranda or I been allowed untrammelled access between house and garden, and, we discovered, nor had most of our other peers. Popsie and I could romp with each other and our newfound friends for hours on end, as long as the weather was good. But even when it was not, John allowed us to come and go as we pleased between the garden and the conservatory, which had sofas and chairs covered in deliciously water-proof plastic. So we would gambol about outside, rolling in the wet grass and generally delighting in the aquatic sensations the rain and soaked plants endowed us with, until we were chilly. Then and only then would we head back inside via the open conservatory door to the attractions of a dry but nevertheless delightfully smelly room where many of the other guests, who were not water dogs like us, would earlier have taken refuge from the rain.

As there was always a full complement of guests — it is astonishing how a doggie hotel with a good reputation functions at an even more optimized capacity than the finest human hotel in the world - we were able to make new friends from all over the place. When I stop to think how often I witnessed disharmony on earth between humans, I am amazed that I never once saw even the slightest hint of trouble between any of the canines in John's hotel. Of course, there were occasional instances when one dog needed to growl a measured warning to another that he or she did not want attention from so and so, or that they were being (hopefully unintentionally) disrespectful and encroaching on one's (temporary) territory, but, aside from those necessary reminders of etiquette, there was not one problem that could have justly been called serious.

This, I suspect, is because John ran a relaxed but nevertheless well-structured show. Each of us had our own feeding bowl which our parents brought with us. We were all fed according to the rules of the Corps Diplomatique, in which the doyen is the longest-serving ambassador and the most junior is the latest comer, irrespective of whether the former is representing an insignificant country like Burkino Fasso and the latter somewhere as powerful as the United States of America. By prioritizing the way he did, John gently but firmly discouraged any attempt to break ranks, which eliminated any potential causes of conflict before they had a chance to develop.

Of course, some dogs are less outgoing than others, with the result that I made friends much quicker than Popsie Miranda. But even the shy dogs at John's hotel would soon be joining in the fun before too long, and my beautiful daughter was by no means so reserved that she wasn't a quick and eager participant as long as the games were to her taste.

The stimulus of all these new friends made for a great atmosphere. It was also a genuine rarity. The only other place I have ever known strange dogs to rub along so well is in Pet Heaven. This is largely because in both places there were no concerns about food.

Of course, in the earthly wild, dogs do encounter a variety of other dogs from different packs. This inevitably results in vociferous warnings that will be followed by fierce fights if not heeded, because in the wild dogs need to protect their territory and food supply against strange packs.

But the way John had things structured, all his canine guests, though initially strangers from different packs, were confident that their food supplies were safe. This freed us all up to enjoy the access we had to a whole range of new friends. And we did make friends with an alacrity I had never experienced before and have never experienced since, except in Pet Heaven, not that I am trying to disparage my life with Ma. Although she did allow us to make friends with other dogs in the park, it was never for very long. Always, we would be called back just as we were really starting to enjoy ourselves – and if she didn't call us back, you can depend upon it, the human parents of our playmate would.

Because of the way John allowed all his guests to mix and mingle, I can truthfully say that I always had such a good time at his hotel that I did not mind being left there in the least. And Ma knew this, not because John or I told her – which I did, but her language skills were not so well developed that she could fully understand the complexities of what I was trying to convey – but because every time she dropped Popsie Miranda and me off we would wag our tails avidly as the car approached his hotel. As soon as we arrived, we would leap out enthusiastically, and run towards his front door yapping out an affectionate hello. This was a tremendous relief to Ma, who was reluctant to leave us with anyone she did not know well, and on the first occasion she was leaving us with John, she kept on telling us that she only hoped that the friend who had recommended him was not exaggerating how much we would enjoy our stay, otherwise she would never forgive herself for allowing us to be placed in an uncomfortable situation.

If our leave-taking from John's lessened Ma's anxieties about our welfare away from her after our first two stays, it was when she came to pick us up at the end of our third visit that she fully appreciated the real pleasure we got from being at his hotel. This was because both Popsie Miranda and I turned back to give John's hand some of the licks which he so enjoyed, prior to jumping into the car. "You girls really do enjoy yourselves there, don't you?" Ma said, the sound and scent of relief suffusing the car. Although Popsie Miranda was never as assertive as I was, even she yapped out so enthusiastic an affirmation that I found myself having to yap louder and longer than I would normally have done. Ma, bless her soul, not only understood, but took the thought a step further: "If you enjoy the company so much, I'm going to see about getting you some of your own."

The following day, I was astonished when Ma telephoned Keith

Butt, the vet who owned the Elizabeth Street Clinic, and offered our flat as a home-away-from-home for dogs. I dashed into the bedroom to wake up Popsie Miranda, who was sleeping peacefully on the three-foot square Persian-rug cushion which Ma had on her bed for us. She wasn't so eager to come and hear the rest of the conversation, but I insisted, so she eased herself off the bed as elegantly as she did everything else, and wiggled beside me all the way down the passage to the sitting room, where Ma was finalizing arrangements with Mr Butt.

The human time line being a much tardier thing than the canine – you might have noticed once we make a decision we act upon it without delay - it wasn't until the weekend that we met the first of our new friends. Webster, a white Scots terrier, came with his human parents to see whether we would all get on. After only the briefest of sniffs, we all decided we liked each other. This was a supreme relief to Charley and Lily, who both worked and had been getting increasingly concerned about leaving their adored boy home alone all day. If they could drop Webster off each morning and pick him up early each evening "that would be ideal. The answer to our prayers," Lily, a nice American in her early twenties married to the charming Englishman who didn't look much older than her, said.

While Ma was working out the logistics of droppings-off and pickings-up with Webster's parents, the doorbell rang. Ma said, "Ah. The other potential friend has arrived," and shot off down the passage to press the intercom buzzer to let them into the building. Within seconds there was a knock on our front door, and no sooner did Ma crack it than a huge golden retriever, who was clearly an overgrown puppy, bounded into the flat, dragging another American lady with him. This time, though, she was a willowy blonde with the looks of a model. Behind her was her husband, another young Englishman who was laughing good-naturedly as his wife apologized for their boy Nosher's high spirits.

"Don't worry, I like enthusiasm," Ma said as he leapt up at her hoping to plant a kiss on her cheek and front paws on her shoulders.

"Nosher, stop that," both Stephanie and Roger said.

But Nosher paid not a blind bit of notice. Within seconds he had toppled Ma onto the floor and was covering her in the most massive licks I had ever seen a dog give a human being. Ma was laughing, but while doing so, she managed to regain control of the situation and was soon telling Nosher that much as she loved affection and enthusiasm, he would have to restrain himself if he wanted to come and stay with us each day while his parents were at work.

As soon as Nosher calmed down a bit, I went up to him, closely followed by Popsie Miranda, and started to sniff him out. Webster soon joined in the introductory ritual, and before too long the four of us had decided that we would get along famously. Which is precisely what we did for the next three or so years.

Of course, having Webster and Nosher to stay on a daily basis was not quite as exciting as staying at John's hotel, if only because the four of us quickly became a settled unit. When Popsie Miranda and I were at John's, we had the delights of unpredictability as well as a larger cast of canines to stimulate us, which does not mean that we did not appreciate Ma's efforts or Webster and Nosher's company, for we did. But variety is the spice of life, and though we would never have wanted to trade being with Ma for a permanent life at John's, nor indeed would we have wanted to share our home and family life with too many other dogs on too constant a basis, the fact is, the best lifestyle would have been if Ma had run a doggie hotel with an ever-changing cast of guests, as well of course as one or two staples such as Webster and Nosher, for four days a week, keeping the other three days free for just the three of us, with morning runs with Pa and Sootie to complete the ideal picture.

Throughout this halcyon period, I can think of only one instance when things were less than ideal for Popsie Miranda and me. This was on 28th July 1991. Ma left us home alone to go to Prince Philip's 70th birthday party at Windsor Castle. As there would be dinner, dancing, Beating Retreat and a fireworks display, that meant she left relatively early and didn't plan to get back home till late.

Because dogs do not react well to fireworks, Ma couldn't take us and leave us in the car the way she normally did. Wrongly supposing that we would be okay since there were two of us to keep one another company, Ma sailed out of the flat with nary a thought to the problems she was inviting.

In fact, two of us meant that we could protest twice as loudly.

To compound her misjudgement, Ma neglected to leave on any lights. Being left alone was bad enough, but, once darkness fell, Popsie

Popsie and I chill in front of the fire in London during the golden period.

Our first major snowfall, which we loved though we couldn't swim in the lake, which was frozen.

Miranda and I really got very spooked at the prospect of remaining in a dark and empty flat.

At first, we tried to occupy ourselves by watching the passing parade on Ebury Street from our vantage point on the sofas. But once night descended, all we were able to see was a conglomeration of shadows. Hardly entertaining and definitely not interesting, I can confirm.

Boredom was now setting in in a big way. "When *is* Ma coming back?" Popsie Miranda asked me anxiously. "She's been gone for an age. Do you suppose something's happened to her?"

"No. She used to do this to me when I was younger," I said. "But she stopped after our neighbour at West Eaton Place complained about the noise I made when she was out."

"Are you saying that she'll have to return if we start barking?"

"Something like that," I replied.

"Well then, let's bark," Popsie Miranda said as she let out the first of a series of barks. I followed these up with some choice ones of my own. One thing led to another and before you knew it, I was giving full rein to my mellifluous vocals, hitting all sorts of notes which transfix humans as well as dogs, while Popsie Miranda excelled herself, sounding like a whole backing chorus instead of the lone treasure she was.

Determined though I was to alert the outside world to the fact that someone had to inform Ma that it was time she returned home, I was not panicking. But Popsie Miranda was. After awhile, she gave way to the fear that Ma might not return in time to rescue her from the terror of human motherlessness. The primitive portion of her personality, which formed the wolf-like foundation of all domesticated canines, now overwhelmed her, so she changed tack and started a howling session that would have turned the young Jamie Lee Curtis green with envy.

As Popsie Miranda's howls resonated with deafening annoyance throughout the neighbourhood, eclipsing my barks (some achievement that!), and making even the Scream Queen's screams sound pleasant, I felt sure it was only a matter of minutes before someone would sit up, take notice, and do something. So I would chill out from time to time, my ears cocked for Ma's return or even the arrival of MacDonald the porter, who had the keys to our flat and would surely let himself in to check on us rather than continue to ignore this kerfuffle. Meanwhile, Popsie Miranda howled away for all she was worth.

Unbelievably, nothing happened for a good two hours. As far as I was concerned, this really was too much, especially when I stopped to think where our flat was located.

Not only were we a complex of four blocks of apartment buildings, but there were two other blocks of flats directly opposite ours, one diagonally opposite, on the corners of Eaton Terrace and Ebury Street, the other facing our sitting room directly on Ebury Street. Both these building were the Police married quarters. If the Police themselves remained deaf to our protests, surely we could not be barking and howling loudly enough. So I encouraged Popsie Miranda to howl with renewed vigour as I cast my mind back to the bad old days at West Eaton Place when Ma used to leave me home alone for hours on end. Surely one of our many neighbours, police or lay, would take exception to the racket and bring our abandonment to a close?

Incredibly, it took until midnight before I heard the key turning in the front door. Behind it I could smell two strange men and MacDonald. The Lord be praised. Help was finally at hand.

MacDonald let the two strange men into the flat. They turned on the lights, looked through the various rooms, and articulated the preposterous notion that "everything is okay", to quote one of them. 'What,' I felt like asking him, 'is your definition of okay?' But I knew there was no point in speaking to him, for his command of Doglish would doubtless be even more inadequate than Ma's. So, instead, I wagged my tail at him to let him know how grateful I was that he had come to rescue us from loneliness and boredom.

My tail evoked the desired response. While he was stroking me, Popsie Miranda sidled up to his colleague and started to lick his hand. He must have been ticklish, for this set him off giggling. Before any of us knew what was happening, Popsie Miranda had jumped up on the sofa and had her forearms resting on his shoulders. She was licking him ten to the dozen, which set him off into even more peals of giggles.

The other policeman started to laugh. "I'll just check that all the windows are secured," he said. "Just in case they were barking to warn intruders off."

Would you believe it, when he reached the bathroom he discovered that the window there, though shut, was not locked. So he turned the key in the lock, told his colleague about it, and concluded with, "We'd better write a note to let their owner know that they're fine. But that we had to come and check on them as the neighbours feared someone had broken in. And the bathroom window wasn't locked." That said, he plucked a piece of notepaper from Ma's desk in the sitting room and started to write on it.

Having completed the task, the two officers gave us last pats, MacDonald let them out of the flat, locked the front door after him, and Popsie Miranda and I were home alone again. This time, however, the lights were on. We also knew someone would come to our rescue if we called them. So, armed with that knowledge, we could be silent in safety and serenity until Ma came back home. Which she did at three o'clock that morning.

You can imagine her consternation when she returned to discover that the Police had come to check up on us. "I really thought you were both mature enough to be left alone just this once, without causing a fuss," Ma said, disappointment oozing out of every pore until she read the note. Ah, how her tune changed as I settled down to enjoy the sweetness of vindication. "I can't believe it. In the five and a quarter years that we have lived here, the bathroom window has never once been locked. Thank God you girls caused a fuss and the Police came. I shudder to think how vulnerable to break-ins we've been all the time we've lived here. I didn't even know the window *could* lock. Or, to put it another way, I thought it was permanently locked and couldn't be opened."

Ma's gratitude was something well worth having. Later, she went to the butcher on Elizabeth Street and got him to sell her two large, marrow-filled bones, which she gave us along with lots of kisses and strokes and a little homily about how someone must be looking out for her. She was still finding it difficult to believe that she had lived for this length of time in a flat with an unlocked window and yet had never been burgled.

If we had one lucky escape thanks to something related to one member of the Royal Family, we were about to have our lives inadvertently endangered by another. It was November 1991. Ma was putting the finishing touches to her latest book. As was her wont, she broke off to let us out for a quick circuit around the apartment building. This always entailed us running into the garden, chasing various scents throughout the rose bushes, and finishing off our perambulations with a variety of sniffs and pees on the grass. These forays were always a pleasure for Popsie Miranda and me and a quick break for Ma, who might otherwise have grown square-eyed in front of the computer.

Our apartment complex, however, possessed a dangerous flaw. In the centre of the four buildings was a parking lot surrounded by a circular driveway. You could gain access to it only through an automated barrier. Because several members of the Government lived in our flats, including a former Prime Minister and various Secretaries of State, and the IRA terror campaign was still at its height, targeting those self-same members of Government past or present, every time one of the Secretaries of State or Ministers of Government was approaching, the security vehicle which invariably preceded his car would raise the barrier, allowing his car to tear into the driveway at speed. On more than one occasion they narrowly missed running over some of the residents' pets, so Ma would never let us out of our building until she could see that the barrier was down and there were no security cars around.

All the residents knew of the problem, so no one save its owner ever opened a door to let out a pet.

Now, you might remember me telling you earlier in this book that our flat was on the ground floor. Facing our front door were two sets of glass doors which provided entry into the building: inner swing double doors, and an outer door about six feet away which you had to open with a key or a latch. This outer door led onto a portico in front of which was the driveway. To the left and right of the portico were shallow steps leading to the garden, but, if we were careless (which we occasionally were), we could easily 'spill' over onto the driveway. With all the dangers pursuant to the secret servicemen using the driveway as a race course, and the circular nature of the driveway enhancing the danger exponentially, Ma would have had to be very careless indeed to ever let us outside without first ensuring that it was safe to do so. Not only was she the antithesis of careless, but she had had a heightened awareness of the danger cars presented to us ever since I had been run over by Pa's friend when I was nine months old.

This evening, however, circumstances in the shape of a little old lady named Queen Elizabeth II conspired to render all Ma's carefulness void when Ma opened our front door.

Normally, I would rush out followed by Popsie Miranda. We would run across the large Deco-style lobby and screech to a halt in front of the inner double swing doors. Ma would then open these and we would rush across to the outer door, once more coming to a sharp halt in front of it, until Ma judged it safe to open it and let us outside.

This evening, however, as soon as Ma opened the door, I clocked an opportunity we had never before had. One of the inner double doors was open, secured by the back of the army officer from upstairs whose wife was one of the Queen's ladies-in-waiting. The Queen was standing between the two sets of doors, shielded by the shut inner door, while her lady-in-waiting was directly in front of her husband dropping a great big leave-taking curtsey to Her Majesty.

Well, I don't know one dog who would fail to take advantage of a gap like that. The mere fact that I would have to screech to one halt instead of two was all the incentive I needed to bolt straight for the outer door, which I confidently expected to remain as shut as it always did.

I reckoned without the thoughtfulness of our dog-loving – and quick-thinking -Queen. Assessing the situation with the celerity that any intelligent human or dog possesses, and being ignorant of the underlying problem caused by the security services, she broke off from receiving the curtsey and leapt to open the outer door for us. As she did so. I rushed through it with Popsie Miranda in close pursuit to the accompaniment of an anguished howl from Ma. She was shrieking something half-way between 'No' and 'don't'. Of course, we didn't pay a blind bit of notice as we rushed straight into the driveway. I swivelled around just as Ma flew past the Queen. This poor lady, who had only been trying to be helpful, had to jump out of Ma's way to avoid being knocked over. Ma, normally so correct, was oblivious to the *lese majeste* of her behaviour as she screamed out to us, "Stop. Stop right this instant. I tell you, stop." Meanwhile, the Queen's face was a picture of mortified concern; for she could see only too clearly the danger she had exposed us to.

All is well that ends well, as the saying goes. Once Ma had called us back, she started to apologize to the Queen for nearly knocking her over, but the dear lady said she could well see why Ma had needed to fetch us back from the driveway. Oozing love from every pore, she then patted us. While she bent over to do so, she was telling Ma how beautiful she had always thought us to be – she was a frequent visitor to our block of flats – and after I gave her a few licks and yaps and Popsie Miranda allowed our sovereign to stroke her, she straightened up to take her leave. As she did so, Ma dropped her own curtsey to the Queen, and while I was wagging my tail at her she hopped into her Jaguar, joining her driver and protection officer who had been sitting quietly in the car amused by the whole doggie fandangle. They left me with no doubt that this was but one of many situations in which England's dog-loving monarch showed an earthiness and

Here I am walking beside the circular driveway that caused such trouble for the Queen and me.

solidity that all politicians should possess.

As we all know, however, life is not always ideal. The first of the big changes which would prove this point came in 1991 when Ma, Popsie Miranda and I stopped going on daily runs with Pa and Sootie. This coincided with Ma finding herself too busy to see Pa each evening after he had finished work, the way they had done throughout our whole lives. There was no row and no real rupture. Ma simply wound things down. Although we missed seeing Pa and Sootie as regularly as we had always done, Ma made the transition as painless for us as possible by retaining sufficient elements of our old schedule for us to feel that our regimen had not changed too much. True, on a daily basis we now went running in Battersea Park instead of Hyde Park, and we did so an hour or so later (Ma hated getting up early, but had done so to oblige Pa), but since we had always gone running in Battersea Park on weekends when Pa was away, even those changes were shifts in emphasis rather than radical departures. And, to give Ma her due, she did ensure that we still went for the occasional run in Hyde Park with Pa and Sootie, though the gaps between the runs went from weeks to months, and before you knew it, Sootie had developed cancer and died, after which Ma stopped taking us for runs with Pa altogether.

The next big change occurred just before Sootie's death. Ma's latest book hit the bestseller list on both sides of the Atlantic. This meant that she had more money than she had ever had before, so she informed us that she planned to invest some of it in a place in the country. She was quite specific about what she wanted. It had to be a wing in a country house that had been converted into flats, so that she could lock it up and leave it without having to worry about burglars. It had to be on the ground floor so that we would have easy access to the grounds, which of course had to be large enough and far enough away from a road so that we could romp without endangering life or limb. And it could be no more than two hours from London, for she had no intention of living there all the time and needed an easy commute.

Ma could be quite doggish at times. One of the characteristics she had in common with us was what I call 'canine implementation'. Once she had made up her mind, she didn't hang about like some of her friends, talking ideas to death rather than acting upon them. She therefore telephoned various estate agents one morning and by the end of that very week we had looked at four different properties. By the end of the second week, we had seen a further eight, and when the third week ended and we were up to twenty, she announced, "The only one I like is the first one I saw. It's the best in every way possible." As indeed it was.

Haresfield Court was a large, Grade 2 listed Jacobean house that had been converted into seven flats. It was situated on the plain at the foot of Haresfield Beacon, an area designated as being of outstanding natural beauty, which overlooked the Severn Vale. The stables had also been broken up into attached houses, though they were far enough away from the Court that you couldn't even see them unless you were looking for them. Not that they were of any interest to Ma. She didn't "like pokey rooms" and adjudged the size of their rooms to be precisely that.

The flat we saw definitely did not have pokey rooms. It took up half of the ground floor of what was a large historic house. There was a spacious, panelled drawing room with a magnificently carved stone fireplace which was itself listed as being of architectural significance; a dining hall; three large bedrooms and a smaller fourth bedroom that overlooked our own inner courtyard; two good sized bathrooms, one of which was en suite with our bedroom; a kitchen and basement, of nearly the same dimensions as the remainder of the flat, which Ma didn't even bother to use except for storage once we bought it.

Haresfield Court was set in several acres of beautifully maintained grounds, hundreds of yards away from the (minor country) road which abutted the adjoining fields which were still farmed. The farmer allowed the residents of the Court to walk in his fields for a fee of £5 per annum (thereby proving himself to be a good neighbour as well as an astute businessman, for by giving us a licence he prevented us from acquiring a right of way over his land), his only other proviso being that we did not disturb his herds of cattle. As Ma liked cows – a species of animal we had never seen before but quickly grew to like, even if they seemed dubious about us and always fled in their version of a mini-stampede whenever Popsie Miranda and I got too close to them – she

I definitely approved of our new country pile.

was always enthusing about the beauty of looking out of her bedroom window past the gardens onto fields where cattle grazed.

England is notorious for the length of time it normally takes to buy property. Six months to a year is the average, but Ma managed to (in the vernacular) 'put in her offer', 'exchange contracts' and proceed to 'completion' within a matter of weeks.

In the interim, she took us to various auctions at Phillips and Bonhams, the auction houses, where she stocked up on antique furniture and rugs. Ironically, she would soon need none of it, for there would be a rash of deaths in her family, which meant that she inherited a whole heap of 'stuff'.

This was a particularly busy period for us. While Ma was equipping Haresfield prior to moving in, she also had to promote her book. For her, that meant trips to places as disparate as the US, Canada, Germany, Italy, even Japan. For us, it meant yet more delightful and stimulating stays at John's hotel.

By far the most momentous change during this period, however, resulted from the marriage Ma arranged between Popsie Miranda and Gimli, a ravishingly beautiful liver and white Springer Spaniel we had met in Battersea Park. This produced five puppies, four boys and a girl. Again, Ma had no choice as to which dog she would keep. I know she was disappointed, for Maisie Carlotta looked nothing like us. Although she was black and white too, where we had large, solid markings, hers were an explosion of more or less uniform speckles. Where we had fairly long and soft hair, her coat was shorter and more bristly. But what upset Ma the most was that Maisie Carlotta did

The fields adjoining the house were great, with or without balloons in the sky.

not share our high and noble foreheads and relatively short snouts, but had the low forehead and longer snout of her paternal ancestors.

"Oh dear," I said to Popsie Miranda. "Here we go again. But you don't need to despair. Ma will come around only too soon, then nothing and no one will be able to shift her love away from Maisie Carlotta."

If Popsie Miranda proved to be as equable as I was about Ma's feelings towards Maisie, she was anything but where sharing her maternal duties with me were concerned. For the first three days after the birth of the puppies, she resisted my advances as I attempted to crawl into the whelping basket and share the joy of breast feeding with her. But Popsie Miranda was a good hearted girl, and when she realized that my milk had also come in and I really needed the release that

Popsie Miranda suckles my grandchildren.

feeding the puppies would bring, she stopped snarling her disagreement and vacated the basket. Thereafter, we shared everything: Not only feeding the puppies, but also cleaning them up and giving them all the love and attention they needed.

By the fifth day, however, it was becoming apparent that one of the little boys was not flourishing. While the other four puppies were growing at what the vet would laughingly call an 'alarming rate', the runt of the litter, always small, seemed to be shrinking. So Ma took him back to the vet, who diagnosed a cleft palate. "He might not survive," he warned her. "Often a cleft palate is indicative of severe internal problems. But even if he has none, he won't survive unless you feed him yourself with a dropper. He doesn't have the ability to suckle, and until he is older and we can see about closing his palate, you will have to feed him around the clock. You should think about putting him down."

"No, no, no," Ma said. "As long as he isn't in pain, I will take care of him."

"You do realize you're not going to get a good night's sleep for the foreseeable future. You'll have to wake up every three or so hours to feed him."

"If that's what it takes, that's what I'll do," Ma said.

She was as good as her word. But nature did not intend this adorable little mite to have a long life, and at four o'clock on the

By the end of the third day, I was suckling the puppies as well.

morning of the seventh day he stopped breathing.

Although Popsie Miranda and I were sad that he had not survived, we were far less upset than Ma, who cried and cried, little understanding that there wasn't that much to cry over, for we would all be linking up some years later in Pet Heaven, and a gap of a few years is like the blink of an eyelid in eternal terms.

The eight remaining weeks that we had all the other puppies flew by, then it was time for us to say goodbye. Popsie Miranda and I knew that our three progeny were going to good homes, so that took some of the sting out of the separation. And our knowledge that we would all be together one day took the rest of it out, though of course we were still sad to say *au revoir*.

Meanwhile, we had a puppy to train. And train Maisie Carlotta we did, though when I say we, I really am being very generous to Popsie, for I, being the top dog, did most of the training myself.

In no time at all, Maisie was properly house trained. She was also incredibly good-natured: loving, gentle, almost as obliging as Popsie Miranda, and even friendlier. Every time she saw anyone – and by anyone I mean both canines and *homo sapiens* – she would greet them enthusiastically then roll over on her back and squirm deliciously until

Maisie Carlotta was a willing pupil.

they rubbed or sniffed her tummy. She quickly chose her daily space, lying beside me and behind Ma while she wrote and Popsie Miranda reposed in her customary place beneath Ma's feet. At night, she had already chosen the one available spot that provided her with untrammelled access to Ma's back. Thereafter, whenever we were ready for bed, she would press herself up against Ma, which on occasion gave

As you can see, my grand-daughter fitted right in without a hitch.

Here I am (on the left) with Popsie Miranda and Maisie Carlotta waiting in our baskets for bickies.

Ma backache, though she never once made her move. As I had predicated, Ma quickly overcame her misgivings about Maisie, and was by this time she was so enamoured of her that she didn't have the heart to stop her snuggling.

It's just as well that Maisie Carlotta grew up as rapidly as she did, for I shudder to think what might have become of Ma's back otherwise. Soon Maisie was so large – far larger than either me or her canine mother – that she could no longer snuggle against Ma the way she used to when she was smaller. This, more than anything else, is what spared Ma from backache thereafter.

If we thought our family had stopped growing at three canines and one human, we were mistaken. A year after Maisie Carlotta's birth, Ma dropped us off at John's hotel for what would prove to be our final visit. When she picked us up two and a half weeks later, she took great pains to inform us that our family had expanded even further. We had two brothers. Human brothers.

Talk about ringing in the changes.

Chapter Seven

Although Ma had warned us that Dmitri and Michael were babies and not puppies, nothing she said could have prepared us for these two strange little mites with fuzzy white down on their heads, tiny bodies with arms and legs which seemed to have minds of their own and chubby little cheeks which housed very efficient sucking pads.

The extent of my knowledge of babies had hitherto been restricted to the many embarrassing occasions when Ma told me to sit quietly while she ooohed and aaahed at strange babies after stopping their mothers on the street so that she could admire these works of art reposing in push chairs or prams. On even rarer occasions she would allow me to sniff Alex, James, and Sophie, the children of her friends Kate and Maggie, for all of ten seconds whenever we 'ran into them', which was seldom enough. But as these encounters were fleeting to say the least, I certainly had no real idea of what babies were actually like. Boy was I about to find out.

For the first few months, the decks were very much stacked in our favour. Dmitri and Michael were too young to do anything but sleep in their cribs and howl for food. This certainly endeared them to me as well as to Popsie Miranda and Maisie Carlotta, for we too possessed healthy appetites and could well appreciate why they would make a fuss when the were hungry. But that aside, they were hardly

Right from the start, I warmed to my human brothers, one of whom is seen here with us in the garden at Haresfield.

presences of any significance in our lives. Even their stabs at consciousness were perfunctory from what I could see, for Ma seemed to expend a lot of energy making funny faces in the hope that she'd get a gurgle of delight in response. And of course, because they were human, their rate of growth was so slow that they remained incapable of the activities that any canine would have taken for granted by the time we had reached their age.

All this changed, however, once they started to crawl. Not only did they now possess the ability to come after us, but they were simultaneously 'developing' interests which were quite surprising. (I am being polite here. They gave a whole new dimension to the word 'invasive'. Being Springer Spaniels, however, we were so accommodatingly good-natured that I didn't even realize the extent of our magnanimity until I came to Pet Heaven and swapped stories of the antics our human siblings used to get up to with the Rottweiler and Alsatian friends I have made here. Did they put me right. There is no way they'd have tolerated one fiftieth of what Maisie and I accepted with such alacrity: Popsie Miranda being another matter entirely.)

Day in, day out, Dmitri and Michael would come after one or all of us and try to hug and kiss us. This was largely good, for we springers are natural love machines. But Ma didn't like us licking their faces,

The boys and us girls got along famously from the very outset. Here we all chill on Ma's bed in London.

though they loved it, so we soon learnt to keep our tongues to ourselves until Ma was out. Then we would go hell for leather, slobbering them with all the kisses they yearned for. They would laugh and laugh and laugh and laugh, sometimes so hard that they started to cry, which always brought their nurse from wherever in the flat she happened to be to break the party up. She would scoop them up, soothe them in the mistaken belief that they were distressed, and reprimand us when all we

Note how the boys emulate us, trying to look out of the windows overlooking Ebury Street the way we used to.

were doing was giving them what they wanted.

Being a thirty-something Jamaican countrywoman of the type which thought that dogs had no feelings or rights, Jennifer had difficulty relating to us as sentient beings like herself. Often she would smack us or push us away forcefully for no reason at all, so you can imagine what she was like when she thought she had one. She was constantly telling us in Jamaican-speak that we were 'dutty' (which we took to mean dirty) and narsey (which clearly meant nasty). Sometimes she even said she felt like 'paisanning' us (presumably that meant poisoning), but we didn't take that seriously. We could tell from her tone of voice and scent that she was terrified of alienating Ma, who she knew loved us passionately.

Ma, mindful of the prejudices that certain country folk suffered from (though she cannot have had any idea of the extent of Jennifer's, otherwise she would never have employed her), had already warned her that "you are to make sure that no harm ever befalls any of the dogs. They mean more to me than anyone or anything on this earth except for my two children. While you are responsible for them, anything, no

Dmitri and Michael were as fascinated by our sometime-guest Nosher as they were by us.

matter how slight, that harms them will result in your immediate dismissal." So we knew that Jennifer would never overstep the mark. But you could tell that there were times when she would dearly have loved to release us into the wild, far far away from our London and Gloucestershire homes.

If Jennifer's attitude was tiresome, the *boys* (as our two brothers soon came to be known by one and all – Popsie Miranda, Maisie Carlotta and I were the *girls*) were normally fun, albeit at times in a challenging way. They were endlessly curious about us, which might have had its downside occasionally, but more typically had a tremendous upside, and I quickly came to the conclusion that all doggies should have human toddler siblings. Dmitri and Michael were forever poking their fingers into our nostrils; opening our mouths to inspect them; trying to grab our tongues; pushing their fingers down our throats to see how far they would go; even pulling our ears and tails to see what would happen. Maisie Carlotta and I never minded any of it, but Popsie Miranda, being the delicate flower that she was, would draw the line very definitely if they encroached beyond her comfort zone. Then she would growl at them, and, if they didn't heed her warning, she would snap at them before walking off with her head held high in the air. Sometimes, I would tell her that she should be more relaxed, but she was having none of it. Once, when Michael tried to push a pencil up her nostril to see how far up it would go, she not only growled at him, but when he persisted in continuing, she snapped at him so definitely that he started to cry. Ma, who happened to be next door, heard the commotion and rushed into the room, to see Michael showering the pencil with his tears.

"What's going on?" Ma enquired of Jennifer.

"Michael push a pencil up Popsie Miranda nose-hole," Jennifer said. "More than one time too. When I tell him to stop, he ignore me. So she snap at him."

I would have expected Ma to remonstrate with my beautiful and sensitive daughter, for the only people Ma seemed to be more protective of than us *girls* was the *boys*. But not a bit of it. Ma said, "Honey, you need to listen to what Popsie Miranda is telling you. When she growls at you. She's warning you not to cross the line. If you ignore her, she has to take sterner measures. You must learn to respect the boundaries of all individuals: canine as well as human. Respect is one of life's great fundamentals. Popsie Miranda has a right to determine her own comfort zone. In future, when she growls at you, you must back off. You don't want her getting so upset with you that she needs to snap at you, do you?"

Whether Michael took notice of Ma's homily, or simple didn't want Popsie Miranda snapping at him again, I do not know, but he

The boys showering Popsie Miranda with attention.

Popsie Miranda leaves Dmitri and me to play a deux.

never did try to push another pencil up any of our nostrils.

It was when our human brothers started to walk that the fun and games really started. They loved nothing more than chasing us in the hope that they'd catch us. When we were outside, at Haresfield in the country or in the park in London, Maisie Carlotta and I would enter into the spirit of things and allow them to both chase and catch us, though Popsie Miranda was a lot less accommodating and would usually run off. She would hide herself away until their nurse had them safely in hand, because they had a habit of gripping the long hair on my and Popsie Miranda's sides (Maisie Carlotta had none) so that we would pull them as if they were sleds. It took quite a few sessions of shaking them off with boundary-inducing growls before they got the message, after which they then tried to hang on to our tails. This was a definite no no, requiring even more intensive growls, but finally, they understood, and thereafter we would happily chase squirrels while the *boys* chased after us.

As they got a bit older, they decided that riding us would be a good idea. Although Maisie Carlotta was a bit dubious at first, and Popsie Miranda said that she was no horse and didn't intend to permit anyone to treat her as if she were one, I found the whole thing great fun from the word go. Once I had trained the *boys* to hug me instead of hanging on using my ears as a bridle, we had such fun playing horsey that Maisie Carlotta had a quick re-think and was soon a welcome fourth in the game. Even Popsie Miranda eventually relented, and while she would only oblige if she were in the right sort of mood, she too enjoyed the occasional horsey session. This was just as well, for this practice continued for the next few years. Literally. And once a little girl called Amy came to live near us at Haresfield Court and there were now three riders instead of two, Popsie Miranda relented even more. More often than she was naturally inclined to do, she entered into the spirit of things and allowed one or another of the kids to ride her, even though one could hardly have accused her on those occasions of displaying anything amounting to enthusiasm. But even a delicate flower like Popsie Miranda was still a Springer Spaniel, and, being one of the most obliging breeds in the animal kingdom, she would oblige

We play horsey.

the kids until her patience ran out. At which point she would shake off whichever one was on her, and amble off to sit quietly on the sidelines while Maisie Carlotta and I took turns compensating for her absence.

Two years older than the *boys*, Amy was a pretty little girl who loved animals. She already had a horse, a donkey, a goat and a parakeet, and as soon as she met us she fell completely in love with us. Ma therefore agreed to give her a puppy from the next litter.

Can you believe my luck, getting caught out like that just as I was about to polish off the leftovers?

By then, Ma had figured out that the way to perpetuate my line was to breed from the youngest of us every five years. "That way there'll be a five year gap, which means that at no time will I have more than four dogs and no fewer than three," Ma said.

As Maisie Carlotta was now approaching her fifth birthday, a series of happy events which humans regard as coincidences, but we in Pet Heaven know is divine reward for efforts well executed, took place. The first of these occurred when the Grosvenor Estate offered to swap Ma's flat on the corner of Eaton Terrace and Ebury Street for a house on nearby Bourne Street. They were replacing all the plumbing in our building, and since Ma had two young children, and the repairs were scheduled to take several months, during which time they would have had to re-house Ma, they took advantage of a house falling vacant on the Estate and offered it to Ma. Of course, she accepted it immediately, for it was more than twice the size of the flat, and had the merit of having none of the restrictions that the flat did.

The main, indeed, only restriction that mattered to Ma was the one involving us. Following the birth of Popsie Miranda's litter, there had been a ruckus when several of her neighbours complained to the Grosvenor Estate about the yapping that the puppies indulged in as

I just loved our new house, which had its own small but sweet garden.

Maisie and Popsie Miranda shortly after we moved into the Bourne Street house.

they grew up and reach the age of separation. After protracted and at times bitter negotiations, during which they tried to force Ma to give up Maisie Carlotta, she agreed not to breed from any of us while living at that flat as long as she could keep Maisie Carlotta. Things now fell into place so smoothly that one could almost detect the hand of destiny. Just before we moved into our new house on Bourne Street, Maisie Carlotta reached what Ma regarded as the optimum marriageable age. Knowing that she could now breed from her, Ma set about finding a suitable mate. She consulted various vets, friends and friends of friends, but seemed satisfied with none of the prospective mates. Finally, serendipity played a part the way it had with my marriage and Popsie Miranda's. One afternoon we were in Battersea Park playing with the *boys* when a beautiful black and white spaniel came bounding up to Maisie Carlotta. After they had sniffed each other out, they started to play. Of course, there was no game that either of our human brothers wished to be excluded from, so Dmitri and Michael bounded over and injected themselves between their sister and her new friend. Needless to say, I wasn't about to let a good game pass me by, so I promptly ran over to them to join in the fun. Even Popsie Miranda, who was walking beside Ma, came over to have a closer look.

Ma could see that we were having the time of our lives, so she stood to one side. Out of nowhere, however, came an attractive forty-something American lady with a chic camel-haired coat and a haircut that Ma recognized as being from one of the top hairdressers. "Rupert, come here," she said trying to sound stern, but failing miserably. "I am so sorry. I don't know what's got into him. He loves kids but this is ridiculous," she continued, addressing Ma while we did our level best to ignore her. "Rupert, stop that and come here." she then said, reaching into the melee to grab her boy by the collar.

"There's no need," Ma said, laughing as the spirit of the occasion infected her. "They're just having fun."

"I know it. I'm glad you do too. Some people feel very threatened by Rupert when he goes up to their children to play. But he loves both kids and other dogs."

"He's very beautiful," Ma said.

"He's from the finest line of American springers," the lady said. "And he has a nature to match. I would dearly love to breed from him, but I don't suppose many people here would want half-American springers."

"He looks the same to me, not that I'm a dog expert. Are they any different from English springers?" Ma asked. Even though I was somewhat distracted by the game we canines were playing with the boys, I could tell by her tone of voice that she had marriage on her mind.

"Not at all, but breeders will be nervous that they'd have problems registering them at the Kennel Club."

"That wouldn't deter me in the least. It's the blood that counts, not whether it's registered. Your boy seems to have a lovely nature," Ma said and introduced herself.

"I'm Cam Van Der Linden," the nice American lady replied, and within the next few minutes she and Ma had exchanged details and agreed that Maisie Carlotta and her son Rupert would be married when her next season came around.

In the meantime, Ma arranged to go on a cruise up the Nile in mid-December 1996 with the boys and their nurse Joyce, who was the dreadful Jennifer's welcome replacement.

As luck would have it, Maisie Carlotta came into season about ten days before Ma was due to leave. This meant that the marriage would have to be consummated while Ma was abroad. She therefore telephoned Cam Van Der Linden and told her that they would have to postpone the marriage. But Cam was made of stern stuff. She wanted one of Rupert's puppies as soon as possible, and wasn't prepared to wait the extra six months that delaying the marriage for another season would have involved. So she invited Maisie Carlotta to spend the week that Ma would be away with her, her husband Henry, and their beautiful boy Rupert.

I know as a fact that Cam Van Der Linden had no idea what she was letting herself in for, for she told Ma so in my presence when we went to pick Maisie Carlotta up after her honeymoon. The Van Der Lindens were one of America's oldest Dutch families. WASP through and through, their house was stuffed full of heirlooms which were collector's items of museum quality. And Rupert and Maisie Carlotta managed to break one of their irreplaceable eighteenth century dining chairs as well as a card table from the same epoch while they were enthusiastically renewing their wedding vows for the only half an hour that Cam and her husband had left them alone for the entire duration of the honeymoon. They also damaged an antique Persian carpet one night when the Van Der Lindens were asleep, as well as other items, but neither Cam nor Henry minded any of the damage in the slightest. "As long as we get pick of the litter, Rupert's son will be worth it," was how Cam put it to Ma.

Cam's benevolence was in marked contrast to the way Popsie Miranda and I were treated while Ma was away. Shadow had offered to keep us at her house, and Ma, deceived by her sweet manner into thinking that she was as nice as she appeared to be, had dropped us off there the night before her departure.

What an ordeal that stay turned out to be. Lazy beyond a fault, Shadow never once took us for a walk, notwithstanding the fact that her house abutted a large and verdant garden square. All she needed to do was let us out her front door and take us across the narrow road which was less than three feet away from her front door. But as far as she was concerned, the cemented courtyard at the back of her house was more than adequate, not only for jobbies but also for walkies. I don't know what was worse: the way she would leave us outside for hours on end in the rain and cold, oblivious to the extreme discomfort she was subjecting us to, or how she kept us inside from early in the evening until the following afternoon, but since I already touched upon our ordeal in the very first chapter of this book, I shall not repeat myself further.

Nevertheless, you can imagine how relieved both Popsie Miranda and I were when we heard Ma's car pull up outside Shadow's house after our week in earthly Purgatory. We were at that front door quicker than you could say boo. When Shadow opened the door, we didn't even wait for Ma to come inside. We bolted straight out the front door, and, after greeting Ma with all the kisses and licks we had saved up for her, we both relieved ourselves beside the car, for of course Shadow hadn't bothered to let us out since early that afternoon, when she took us back inside so Ma wouldn't see us cold and wet, and thereby figure out how she had mistreated us.

Our behaviour caused Ma to ask Shadow if we were all right, for our bowels normally did not move at that time of the day, but Shadow had one of her plausible explanations ready, assuring Ma that we had not only been regular as clockwork but no trouble at all and "as well behaved as they are with you."

Having had more than an elegant sufficiency of Shadow, I leapt into the car without further ado. Popsie Miranda followed on my heels literally. Did it feel good to be back on our own terrain! And to be with our two brothers, who were waiting for us with big grins and lots of strokes and kisses. Even to see Joyce, their new nurse, who might not have been a great dog lover but was a kind and decent person so always treated us well if a bit distractedly. What a welcome change from the week in Shadow's rung of hell.

On the way back to Chelsea to pick up Maisie Carlotta, I did my level best to tell Ma about the dreadful time we had had. But Doglish was never her strong point. While she could understand simple concepts such as "I am hungry" or "I want to be let out", anything too intricate was lost upon her. So yet again she got the entirely wrong end of the stick and kept on telling me how pleased she was that I had been such a good girl and behaved myself so well and given Shadow no trouble, which was all perfectly true, but nowhere near the point I was trying to make.

Fortunately, we dogs have an inbuilt tolerance of the human inability to comprehend our language, so once I had had my say, I settled down without frustration to the sheer delight of basking in my family's love. Taking my customary seat between Ma and Popsie Miranda, I let her rabbit on while I shot affectionate looks at her between checking out the welcome sights that London has to offer at all times.

After about twenty minutes, Ma's car pulled up outside Sloane Court West in front of the Van Der Linden's house. As soon as Ma opened her door, I shot out with her, so eager was I to see Maisie Carlotta. She was equally eager to see me, for as soon as Cam opened the door, she was outside licking me, her tail wagging forty to the dozen.

"Maisie has been happy as a clam with us," Cam said, "but I think she'll be happy to return home now. Today is the first day she's not welcomed Rupert's attentions, which I know means her season is coming to an end."

As Ma entered the house to collect Maisie's bowls and basket, Cam started to regale her with stories about the stay. When she came to the part about how they had broken the chair and the card table, Ma was anything but amused, and apologised profusely while offering to help pay for the repairs. But Cam was graciousness and fragrance itself, and I knew then and there that any puppy of Maisie Carlotta's that she had would be a lucky boy indeed to join such a loving home.

Chapter Eight

That year, Christmas came and went like most of the others had done since the *boys* had come into our lives. We spent it down at Haresfield, which of course Santa flooded with presents for the *boys* and us *girls*. While my human brothers played with their new presents, especially the aeroplanes which actually flew, and the battery-powered vehicles they drove in the corridors or outside in the grounds when the weather permitted, for once we *girls* preferred to stay inside. This was because we could safely exercise our jaws with endless bones and treats such as doggie chocolates without having to worry about another dog picking up their scent and coming after them. Millennia of experience had taught us that the only way to keep treasures safe was to bury them. Year after year Ma would let us out with our new chewy treats and squeaky toys then wonder where they had disappeared to, but this year she caught Popsie Miranda burying the most delightful squeaky mouse. Finally cottoning on to what was happening, she gave up asking why our Christmas presents always disappeared, and let us stay inside.

The day after New Year's Day, the whole family returned to London. This was because the *boys* had been going to kindergarten in Eaton Square for the last year, and now that the new term had begun, we were once more restricted to weeks in London and weekends in the country. This, I don't mind telling you, could be a real bore, for while

Here I am inside enjoying some of my Christmas treats with Popsie Miranda.

we *girls* were often in the grounds at Haresfield summer or winter, in London our forays outside were limited to quick pit-stops in the back garden or our daily runs with Ma in Battersea Park.

That January we missed one of our usual weekends in the country because Ma had to attend a party in London to celebrate Chinese New Year on the Saturday evening. Because it was a gloriously warm and sunny Monday afternoon, Ma made up for our lack of fresh air by taking us to the park with the *boys* and their nanny Joyce, who often went there after school. (Battersea Park was a five minute drive from our house.) The occasion turned out to be such a success that Ma took us again to the park the following afternoon. This time though she dropped all of us off and returned home to write.

Over the next few weeks, a new regimen evolved. If the weather permitted, Ma, Joyce and we *girls* would hop into the car when it came time to pick my human brothers up from school. Once classes were over, we would all head to Battersea Park, where Ma would leave us for an hour or two.

Although circumstances prevented Maisie Carlotta from joining us after February, as spring approached and the days lengthened, the rest of us looked forward to this fun time. Joyce and the *boys* would use the play area nearest the Battersea side of the park, while Popsie Miranda and I would stay nearby playing or just chilling. We were so well behaved that it never once occurred to any of us to run off. Which was just as well, for had we done so, we might not have been in the position to save Dmitri.

It was the beginning of April 1997; one of those glorious spring afternoons which are so much remarked upon in London. Although not exactly warm in the shade, it was so sunny that it was warm everywhere else, especially in the play area where the *boys* were on the swings and Joyce was chatting to one of the other nannies with whom she had made friends over the previous months.

For the past week, a sallow, pasty-looking, funny-smelling fortysomething-year-old man with lank hair and sunken eyes had taken to sitting on the perimeter watching the children play. He was always alone and, if you did not know better, you would have thought that he was one of the parents watching his child. Except that he was not.

Because there were seldom fewer than ten and sometimes as many as twenty children - though today there must have been about thirty, for it really was a glorious day and the one time you can count on the English being out of doors is when the sun is shining – it was not obvious that he did not belong. But there was something about his scent that alerted me and Popsie Miranda to the fact that he was not to be trusted, so one of us always kept an eye on him.

Dmitri, Michael, Popsie Miranda and I in Battersea Park just after I foiled the abduction.

Although I did not

know it at the time, he had also aroused the suspicions of some of the nannies, Joyce included. They too were surreptitiously keeping him in their sights, though humans are really not as dogged as dogs, as events would prove.

I was standing watch when I saw the man get up from the grass verge where he was sitting. Michael had just run off to play with a little friend, leaving Dmitri on his own. Normally, this would not have been a cause for concern, but because of the strange man, I was alert to anything that made any of the children in the play area vulnerable. Instinctively, I knew – just knew – that it was they that he was targeting.

He started to pad slowly, too slowly, like an animal stalking its prey before moving in for the kill. He took something out of his pocket and peeled it, replacing the wrapper in his trouser pocket. I could smell that it was a strawberry lollipop. I looked over to where Popsie Miranda was sitting and yapped at her gently. Now that the two of us were facing the danger together, I felt a lot better. If two humans against one is murder, two doggies against a human must surely be instantaneous annihilation.

This weedy man, so insignificant in every way that he would have blended unnoticed into just about any background, then did the most surprising thing. He passed three pretty little girls, two blondes and a brunette with waist-length hair, and went to lean against a pole near to where Dmitri was standing. He waved the lollipop rhythmically in Dmitri's direction.

You could tell that my little brother had not yet seen the man. Instead, he was momentarily at a loss as to what to do. You could almost see him asking himself: 'Shall I run over to Michael, or shall I give brotherly love a break and play with one of my friends?'

As I looked from Dmitri to the strange man, I could see that he was quietly, unobtrusively, almost invisibly, looking directly at my baby brother while the lollipop was doing a dance of its own. It was as if he was willing Dmitri to catch his eye. Which Dmitri did.

Now, my darling brother was very outgoing. Although he and Michael had both been warned by Ma never to go anywhere with strangers, they were both really too young to understand the danger.

And Michael, frankly, was not sufficiently outgoing to allow any stranger to inveigle him into even saying hello; not unless Ma or Joyce were right beside him. But Dmitri was another matter altogether. Not only did he have an inviting disposition, but he also had inviting looks. Blonde, brown-eyed, and cherubic, he had a sturdy, muscular little body that foretold the rugby-player he would grow into.

I saw the moment Dmitri's eyes locked with this terrible man's. He subtly took a small step towards my brother, waving the lollipop almost unobtrusively. Dmitri stepped towards him, his little face a veritable picture of innocent openness. As if by magic, the man closed the distance between himself and Dmitri so quickly and smoothly that it was done in one blink of an eyelid. He accomplished this so covertly and quietly, in fact so silkily, that I was not surprised to see that none of the adults surrounding us had even noticed what was happening. Then he performed another feat. In full view of everyone, he somehow managed to engage Dmitri in conversation, doing so with such stillness and quietude that it was almost as if his actions were muffling what people should observe.

Now, dogs are not stupid. We also have the advantage of having senses that are far more heightened than humans. Even a stupid dog would have realized that something was amiss. And, whatever I am, I was never stupid. So I sat bolt upright, my ears, eyes, nose all twitching at optimum capacity. Watching, waiting, sensing.

I could hardly believe my eyes when I saw this man hand Dmitri the lollipop. My sweet, obedient, candy-loving brother, having been told by Ma never to accept anything from strangers, resisted for all of ten seconds before licking it with relish.

I was just starting to hope that this would be the end of the encounter when I saw the man bend down and point out something in the distance to Dmitri. My little brother turned, looked, nodded his head in agreement, and before I could even blink, the man had taken his hand and was walking away from the play area with him.

This, I knew, was highly irregular, so I did what anyone with two grains of sense in their head would do. I ran over to Dmitri to find out why he was leaving.

Dmitri greeted me, as he always did, with a hug and a kiss. He introduced me to this man, who was bombarding my nostrils with some pretty inappropriate odours. Intermingled with anxiety and fear were lasciviousness and lust, and since I had never encountered anyone in the whole of my life who had this range of odours around children, I was now sure that my little brother had got himself involved with someone who did not wish him well. My instincts turned out to be only too accurate, for, instead of patting me nicely the way most other people did, the man pushed me away with his foot.

"Let Tum Tum come with us," Dmitri said.

"He can't," the man said. "There's no space for dogs there (where we are going)."

"He's a she," Dmitri said.

"Well, *she* can't come," the man said, his voice betraying irritation.

"But she loves going everywhere with us," Dmitri said as the man dragged him away with not so much force that the child would be frightened, but enough to pull him in the direction he wanted to head.

"She'll spoil our treat," the man said as Dmitri looked behind him towards me.

No. This was not right. Ma would be furious when she discovered that Dmitri had gone off with a strange man, especially one who had such a tremendous range of odoriferousness. Even though my little brother did not realize that he was in danger, I could tell that this man meant him no good. So I started to bark. And bark. And bark. This drew Popsie Miranda's attention, who had been keeping watch on the other side of the play area. She ran towards us, stopping just behind me.

Meanwhile, I had resolved not to let Dmitri out of my sight, so I ran back to my brother's side and trailed him as I growled at the man.

He now lost patience with me and kicked out at me, narrowly missing my bad leg. He was hissing that I was to leave them alone. We were now pretty close to the car park so I stuck as close to Dmitri as glue does to paper, howling as well as growling while doing so. This made the man kick at me yet again, which was a big mistake, for this mistreatment upset Dmitri, who reprimanded him in the most earnest of four-year-old tones, "You are being mean to Tum Tum. Stop it or I won't go with you."

With that, the man gathered Dmitri up into his arms. He gave one more kick in my direction before striding off at a very brisk and purposeful pace towards the car park. Dmitri now saw that the man whom he had thought of as nice was anything but. He promptly started to cry and demanded to be put down. But the man was having none of it. I could not stand by and let him take away my little brother without doing something to stop him, so, as Dmitri wriggled trying to get free of his captor, I sank my teeth into the man's left heel. This caused him to flay out at me, but in so doing, he loosened his grip on Dmitri, who somehow landed upright on the ground. By this time, he was crying hysterically. I clung for dear life onto the man's heel as he dragged me across the park with Popsie Miranda growling ominously at him beside me. Then I realized that he was trying to run away from both of us as well as Dmitri, who was now collapsed on the ground some way behind us sobbing uncontrollably. Then, and only then, did I let go of the interloper's heel, at which point he took off like a bat from hell.

Just then, Joyce came running up with Michael in her arms and two of the other nannies. One of the mothers had become aware of what was happening and had alerted her, so she had set off in hot pursuit. She ran towards Dmitri and, lifting him to her ample bosom, hugged him while she and Michael tried to console him.

The man, meanwhile, had run into a clump of trees on the perimeter of the park. Obviously, he was intent on making his escape before anyone could detain him. Which would certainly have happened had he not scampered when he did, for within minutes the Police, whose station in the park was only a few hundred yards away, were tearing up to us in their car, their siren blaring away for all to hear. Someone had telephoned them to tell them a child was being abducted.

After the Police had taken statements from Joyce and some of the other nannies and mothers and spoken to Dmitri, they telephoned Ma. I would have expected her to arrive in a flap, but she was uncharacteristically calm when she showed up. This told me what had happened was very serious indeed, for the only time that Ma failed to be effusive was when she needed to keep all her wits about her. That, plus the fact that our Jaguar tore into the Police parking lot at such a speed that she would indubitably have been prosecuted for speeding if the situation hadn't warranted her breaking the speed limit in full view of the Police.

After Ma had greeted all of us, she listened to the Police recount how Dmitri had nearly been abducted. The way Joyce and the other nannies had reworked the story, they had figured in Dmitri's rescue as prominently as I. Of course, I knew that to be a fallacy, but there was no possibility of my informing Ma to the contrary. Her Doglish just wasn't good enough. But I was pleased to see that even in this fantastical account, everyone acknowledged the crucial role I had played in preventing the abduction. But for me following that awful man and sinking my teeth into his heel, there is no telling what dreadful fate would have befallen Dmitri. The only certainty is that I had foiled a serious crime, and my reward, aside from the many hugs and kisses I got from the *boys* and Ma, was for her to stop off at the pet shop in Pimlico en route to the house. There, she bought more treats for me than any of us had ever received before. Then, when we got home, she saved me the trouble of having to tell Maisie Carlotta and the puppies about what had happened in too much detail, for she spread such an array of chews and bones before us that they all knew instinctively that something momentous had happened and that they were sharing in my reward.

As you can imagine, Maisie Carlotta regretted not being there to back up Popsie Miranda and me, but she was as pleased as can be that the rewards extended to her and the puppies, who were receiving their first taste of what manna from heaven could be like. Ma, being a firm believer in spreading joy around and leaving no one out, had not only bought me more treats than I ordinarily had even at Christmas, but had also purchased a similar amount for all the other dogs. Even the puppies had their mini-versions of our chews, which they masticated upon eagerly until they too were thoroughly exhausted and actually fell asleep with chews beside their little mouths.

Chapter Nine

There was a good reason why Maisie Carlotta was not in Battersea Park with us while I was foiling Dmitri's abduction.

Within weeks of her honeymoon, it had become apparent not only to me and to Popsie Miranda but also to Ma that my beloved granddaughter was pregnant. Day by day her girth expanded so much that I was sure her litter would be a large one. Despite this, she was far more robust than Popsie Miranda had been while expecting her, and she remained as delightfully rough and tumble as she had been before her pregnancy. This meant that she and I could continue being rambunctious on our runs; Popsie Miranda being the angel who could invariably be found beside Ma's ankle. It also meant that she could continue playing with the *boys*, though Ma had to warn them against riding her.

Incredibly, they listened, and even started to fasten their cheeks to her tummy in the hope of detecting movement from the foetuses. You should have seen their little faces when their efforts met with success. They were so jubilant that you would have thought no four year old boy had ever before felt puppies moving in the womb, which of course those two hadn't. "Let me feel," the one who had not heard would beseech, burying his little face in Maisie's side. I was constantly amazed at how patient they would then be until they detected the next bout of movement. Truly, the wonders of nature bewitched them; nothing else seemed capable of keeping them still.

As Maisie Carlotta's due date approached, Ma prepared her whelping basket in a quiet corner of the kitchen away from all draughts and human traffic. This was the same whelping basket that Popsie Miranda and I had had, and it brought back lovely memories. I hoped that my milk would come in the way it had the time before, but of course one has no guarantees about these things, so I would just have to wait and see.

A day or two after Ma prepared the whelping basket – "early just in case", as she put it – Maisie Carlotta's due date dawned. It was Tuesday, 18th February 1997. Would today be the day? We all hoped so, because Maisie Carlotta was so huge that she looked as if she was about to burst. Yet incredibly, she had gone to the park that morning, and while I wouldn't exactly call what she did running, she was certainly going at a faster rate than mere walking.

That afternoon, her breathing quickened. Although Maisie Carlotta had never been in labour before, she knew what it meant. So did Ma, Popsie Miranda and I, who were now dab hands at whelping, having been through it as often as we had. Despite this, Ma was anything but complacent. She telephoned Simon at the Elizabeth Street Veterinary Clinic to put him on notice in case anything went wrong.

When none of the puppies had been born after dinner, Ma telephoned Simon again, only to be told that there was no need for anxiety. There was still plenty of time. So, after the *boys* had had their baths that evening, we all settled down to watching television on Ma's bed until it was their bed-time. When that came and went and Maisie had still not given birth, Ma took us outside into the back garden for a quick pit stop before taking us back upstairs to await developments.

Although the labour was proceeding apace and Maisie was clearly not in any distress, Ma was sufficiently concerned to telephone Simon to find out if it was safe for her to go to sleep. "Yes," he informed her, so she moved the whelping basket from the kitchen to her bedroom, where we settled down for the night.

Ma must have fallen into as deep a sleep as I did, for she started so suddenly at five o'clock in the morning that I too woke up out of a deep slumber. Maisie Carlotta was on the floor panting beside us as if her life depended on it. "I'm sorry, I think this labour has gone on long enough," Ma announced. "I don't care whether it's natural or not, I'm not taking any chances in case you get so tired you become too weak to deliver those puppies. Come, Maisie, we're going to Elizabeth Street for you to get an injection to speed things up."

Within a minute, Ma had hauled on a track suit, grabbed her handbag and glasses, which she had to wear when she did not have in her contact lenses, and was running downstairs closely followed by a bloated and waddling Maisie Carlotta. I could tell she was pleased that Ma was intervening, not because her life was in danger, but because, strong as she was, she was starting to get tired.

They returned to the house fifteen minutes later, after the night-duty vet had given my lovely grand-daughter an injection to quicken delivery. It certainly worked a treat, for Maisie Carlotta didn't even make it back up to her whelping basket in the bedroom. On the mezzanine landing leading from the sitting room up to our bedroom, she paused momentarily. Popsie Miranda and I overtook her. Lo and behold, by the time I looked back from the upstairs landing, out had popped a puppy.

"What a clever girl you are," Ma said in that joyous, intense way she had whenever something wonderful happened. A second later, she had scooped up the puppy, removed its cowl, cut the umbilical chord by squeezing it between two fingers, then handed it to Maisie Carlotta, who was lying between the curtains underneath the window, eagerly awaiting her firstborn.

As I looked down at my granddaughter giving my eldest great-grandchild its first licks prior to settling it onto the breast, I felt a powerful surge of joyousness. Not only was I witnessing the marvel of yet another generation of descendants, but the sheer miracle that is birth filled me with awe and wonderment. Fortunately, being a canine I didn't have to struggle with disbelief or cynicism the way many humans do. I could enjoy the moment for what it was. And did I!

Not, it has to be said, that Maisie Carlotta was exactly appreciative of my efforts when I bounded down the stairs for a closer inspection. I also wanted to give her my help and assistance the way I had given Popsie Miranda when she was born. So I tried to give the puppy a welcome sniff as a precursor to a proper snuggle and maybe even a suckle or two. But Maisie growled ominously, letting me know in no uncertain manner that she expected me to keep my distance. Because I understood that she was following her natural instincts and being protective, I wasn't offended. But I did so want to share some of the love which had filled my heart to overflowing. So rather than turn tail and head back upstairs, I hovered rather precariously on the edge of the landing, squeaking out a pointless supplication that Maisie Carlotta just ignored until Ma intervened saying, "Come upstairs with me, Tum Tum. Maisie doesn't want you here. Remember how it was with Popsie Miranda. Give things a day or two and I'm sure she'll let you in."

By the time the Van Der Lindens came to see the puppies at seven o'clock that evening, all of them had been born. You didn't need olfactory sensors like mine to sense how much they loved the puppies. The way they cooed as they held each and every one, rubbing them against their cheeks, kissing them, sniffing them, would have convinced even the stone-hearted that we were in the presence of genuine dog-lovers. "Oh, I would so love it if Rupert could see his children," Cam said.

"I suppose there won't be much danger of infection as long as they're being breast-fed," Ma said, believing that the puppies would be protected by Maisie's antibodies which they would imbibe through her breast milk.

"Go bring him in," Cam said to her husband before Ma had a chance to change her mind.

What a mistake. No sooner did Rupert come bounding in through the door than Maisie Carlotta was standing in the whelping basket snarling at him.

You could tell he didn't really believe that the Maisie Carlotta, who had been such an enthusiastic wife, would now really exclude her husband from seeing the fruit of their love. Wagging his tail good-naturedly, he edged towards her, which was the second mistake of the evening, for with one leap Maisie Carlotta flew across the room and stood no more than an inch away from him, skinning her teeth and growling ferociously. Her message was unmistakable, so poor Rupert tucked his tail between his hind legs, and backed off with a symphony of apologies delivered in the most gentlemanly whine possible.

These were of no import whatsoever to Maisie, who would not return to her basket until his father had taken him out of the room and Ma had shut the door after them.

Once order had been restored, Ma let Henry Van Der Linden back into the room while Rupert stood at the other side of the door sending us plaintive messages about how much he wanted to see his children. When he realized that nothing he said or did was going to change things, he became quiet, which was just as well, for this was the very moment when his parents were taking their pick of the litter.

Fortunately for Ma, like Popsie Miranda's mother-in-law Nicky, they wanted only a male. After much ooohing and aahing, they chose the most beautiful of all the puppies: a magnificent black and white boy whose markings were similar to Popsie Miranda's and who had my face and forehead. He would grow into such a stunning- looking dog that people would often stop the Van Der Lindens to ask where they had got him.

Once the Van Der Lindens had left, our household settled down to the rhythm that newborns always impose upon their environment. And so things continued for the following two days, with Maisie growling at both Popsie Miranda and me whenever we came near the puppies. But Ma had been right about her letting me into the whelping basket. By the third day, she had relented enough to allow me good sniffs. And by the end of that day, she actually stepped aside and let me settle into the whelping basket with the puppies.

Sadly, I was not able to help her the way I had helped Popsie Miranda when she had had her litter. Notwithstanding my desire to feed my great-grandchildren or their determined suckling on each of my many breasts, my milk stubbornly refused to flow. "Tum-Tum, it's anno domini," Ma finally said by way of explanation, giving me consolation pats at the same time. Of course, I couldn't speak Latin, not

Popsie Miranda and I tend to our descendants.

having been to a good school like Ma. But I nevertheless managed to figure out that "anno domini" referred to my great age of 12, which all dog lovers know to be 84 years old in human terms.

Disappointing as that was for me, it was also dreadful for Maisie Carlotta. There was no way that Popsie Miranda could have helped her even if she had been so inclined. She had had all her left breasts removed after Ma had felt a lump in one of them on New Year's Eve 1994, and the exploratory biopsy had come back positive for cancer. Although Ma wanted John, our vet in the country, to remove all the right breast tissue at the same time "as a precaution", he explained that dogs have so much more breast tissue than humans that there was no way she could tolerate a double mastectomy simultaneously. So Ma waited until Popsie Miranda had recovered before pressing John to remove what he thought was healthy tissue. "Removing all the right breast tissue is very radical," John had said, but Ma was adamant. "Nothing is more radical than death and I'm not prepared to allow its possibility to be factored into the equation. Her grandmother died of breast cancer and the remaining breast tissue is a host if she has a genetic defect. Remove it all."

If Ma's cautiousness seemed extreme before the surgery, once John opened her up he realized how lucky Popsie Miranda had been to have

Popsie Miranda recovers from her first mastectomy.

such a determined mother. Deep within her breast tissue, ready to spread inwards to her vital organs, were a series of pre-cancerous cells and small tumours. "Your instincts have saved her life," John had the good grace to tell Ma when we went to pick Popsie Miranda up after her second mastectomy.

Michael and Dmitri would rush home from school to play with Maisie Carlotta's puppies.

With neither Popsie Miranda nor me in a position to provide extra teats, poor Maisie Carlotta was stuck with the sole responsibility of feeding her brood. And what a brood it was. Nine large and beautiful puppies, all pictures of good health, with not one flaw amongst them. Three were tricolours: black, white and brown. Four were black and white. And two were liver and white. My heart went out to Maisie Carlotta. She could get no peace. She was feeding those puppies around the clock. Although she was a willing and attentive mother, I could tell that she was struggling through exhaustion. All that suckling and eating on demand, so that her body would provide enough milk to feed the puppies, was very hard work indeed.

Although my poor granddaughter was having difficulty coping with the puppies' demands, the *boys* had a great time with them. From the very day of their birth, Ma had showed our human brothers how to hold the puppies so that they could enjoy them without hurting them. Every morning when Dmitri and Michael got up, they headed straight for the whelping basket and the puppies. As soon as they returned from school in the afternoon, they took up their positions beside the basket again, stroking and kissing the puppies for hours on end. I was amazed that children as young as they were did not get bored, much less that they could be as gentle and thoughtful as they were.

Ma was a great believer in love. She often said, "Love is the most important thing in life." She felt it was important that the *boys* be allowed from a young age to experience the delights that the newly-born brought. This, she felt, would convert into a free and easy relationship with the puppies. I don't know how many other mothers would allow their four year old sons into a whelping basket, but I can tell you, the way the *boys'* hearts and pores opened up whenever they

Dmitri and I rest with Popsie Miranda (left) after her second mastectomy.

were sitting in it with the puppies, made me realize that Ma had done the right thing. Their pores poured out the fragrance of pure love, and never once did they abuse the trust she placed in them. Even when she wasn't there to oversee what was happening.

Life, however, is never a one-sided coin. Lurking in the shadows was trouble. The problem was that Maisie Carlotta litter was too large for her to cope with. Vets say that nature has a way of taking care of litters that are too large. While I do not know if I can bring myself to agree with that observation, the fact is that four days after the puppies were born, Ma woke up to see that one of the tricolours had died during the night. She promptly telephoned Simon, who explained that it was relatively common in large litters to lose a puppy a few days after birth.

"But he was perfectly all right last night," Ma said disbelievingly.

"It's not at all uncommon."

Although Ma wanted to take the puppy round to the veterinary surgery for him to do an autopsy to see what the cause of death had been, he assured her there was little point.

Two afternoons later, Ma discovered a second puppy dead. This time it was one of the liver and white boys. He had been a picture of good health earlier that day, so this time she took the puppy around to the Elizabeth Street Surgery with Maisie Carlotta.

"He's been crushed," Simon told her.

"What do you mean: crushed? How crushed?" Ma asked in horror.

"There's only so much space, and if all the puppies are competing for the breast, and huddling for warmth beside the mother, things like this happen," he explained.

"What can I do?" Ma wanted to know.

"Short of creating a larger space than the whelping basket, and sleeping with them at night, there's very little you can do," Simon said.

If he thought Ma would take that recommendation lying down, he didn't know our mother as well as I did. As soon as she returned home, she packed away the whelping basket. She created a new and larger 'nest' for Maisie Carlotta and the puppies beside the kitchen, laying down bedding so that they would be warm against the tiles. When our bedtime rolled around later that evening, after she had let us out for our midnight walk, Ma settled Maisie Carlotta in her new 'nest' then took Popsie Miranda and me upstairs to the bedroom. We settled down on the bed in our customary places while Ma went to the bathroom to wash off her make up and brush her teeth as usual. This night, however, would prove to be anything but typical, for rather than re-join us as she normally did when she had finished, Ma poked her head round the door and said, "Good night, girls. I'm going to sleep with Maisie Carlotta and the puppies. I'll see you in the morning."

If I could hardly believe my ears, my eyes were also presented with an incredible sight the following morning when a bleary-eyed Ma staggered upstairs. "Every time Maisie Carlotta moved, I checked to see that the puppies were all right. Although I did get some sleep, I can't say I got very much," Ma said. "But it's been worth it. All the puppies are fine."

Glad as I was to hear it, I hoped she wouldn't be too tired for a nice, long run in the park. Fortunately, she wasn't. Popsie Miranda, Maisie Carlotta and I had a fine old time that morning, after which Ma took us back home and promptly fell into bed, giving a mean approximation of a prone statue fir the next few hours.

She arose to discover that the largest of the puppies, a magnificent tricolour whom she had nicknamed Il Magnifico, was lying limp in the whelping area. Although he was breathing, it was obvious something was radically wrong. So she scooped him up, wrapped him in one of her sweaters, and took him straight to the Elizabeth Street Clinic. There, she discovered that her efforts the night before had yielded slim returns, for he had been crushed while she was asleep upstairs. "Simon says that he'll survive if he lives long enough to be able to wriggle away when he's being crushed, but that he might never be fully all right. He suspects he's been brain damaged as a result of oxygen deprivation," Ma explained when she returned home.

For the next week, Ma not only slept with Maisie Carlotta and the puppies at night, but she watched them like a hawk during the day as well. I don't know where she got the energy from, but she was determined to see that neither Il Magnifico nor any of the other puppies would be crushed until they were big enough to survive.

By the end of that week, however, it was obvious that Il Magnifico was not flourishing. Where formerly he had been the largest of the puppies, he was putting on so much less weight than the others that he was now in danger of becoming the smallest. So Ma took him back to Simon in the hope that he could provide supplements. These, however, made no difference, and a few days later he entered Pet Heaven while Ma was stroking him in the palm of her hand.

Although the *boys* and we *girls* were saddened by his early departure from this earth, Ma was disconsolate. I tried to point out to her that we would meet him again soon enough, and she must be more canine about separations such as death, but once more her limited language skills prevented her from understanding what I was saying. But she did understand the licks and kisses and snuggles which I gave her, and she hugged me and told me how lucky she was to have such beautiful babacitas (her pet word for her dogs) as us – and me in particular.

Despite her sadness over the loss of Il Magnifico, Ma still had much to be happy about. There were six robust puppies remaining, and, because none of the black and whites had died, she retained the unprecedented luxury of being able to choose which puppy she wanted to keep from amongst them. Although she was now nervous that the puppy she had chosen and named Maud Livilla in honour of her beloved great-aunt Maud would not survive, she got over that fear when Maud grew large enough to wriggle away from the heaviest of live weight.

The survivors certainly were beautiful.

How I loved the time I spent with my great-grandchildren.

By the time the puppies had received their second lot of vaccinations, they were so large that there was little doubt that all would survive. Ma now had the task of finding good homes for them. "Always a bitter sweet experience," she used to say, explaining how happy she was to give other people the chance to enjoy having a puppy, even if it was always heart-wrenching to part with her 'grandchildren'.

Finding 'good homes' for puppies was an intense affair fraught with potential dangers. This made the exercise both poignant and exciting.

Dmitri and Michael loved the puppies too.

Grant comes to collect Molly.

As each prospective parent came to choose a puppy and be given the third degree by Ma in a charming manner that was no less penetrating for being conducted with a patina of civility, I felt my blood pressure rise commensurate with that of the interviewee and interviewer.

With such conflicting emotions as hopefulness, fear, love, sadness, expectancy and anticipation spraying the air with their pungent scents, I could well see why Ma called the process bitter-sweet.

What consoled her somewhat was that two of the puppies were going to great friends. The first, a beautiful liver and white girl, joined an all male household, bringing the feminine touch to Bertie and Ogilvy, and Grant and Roger. The second went to our Haresfield neighbours whose daughter Amy had become a great friend of the *boys* by this time. They chose a magnificent black and white puppy whom Amy wanted to call Cruella, in honour of the character from 101 Dalmatians. Fashion or no fashion, there was no way I wanted any descendant of mine to be named after a monster, fictional or factual. So

The Lady Constance Pruella de Vil with Linda.

I barked out a very firm protest, which Ma fortunately agreed with.

"I tell you what, Amy," Ma said in her diplomatic tone of voice which I knew meant she meant business and you'd better not oppose her, otherwise she'd start the human equivalent of barking, "why don't we compromise? I'll name her The Lady Constance Pruella de Vil in honour of you and your choice, for you are a nice young lady and so is she and you can call her Pruella for short." Amy agreed, and within days of taking possession of the puppy, she was calling her Pru, so all ended well there.

Meanwhile, something happened to turn the process entirely sour insofar as we dogs were concerned. Shadow asked if she could have the only remaining tricolour, whom Ma had nicknamed Minette, Citoyenne de France in honour of the French national flag. She was spectacularly beautiful and two of Ma's other friends had already asked if they could have her. "She's so sweet and I feel the need to have something to love aside from Kevin," Shadow said about her boyfriend in that saccharine-laden but emotion-free voice of hers.

I could hardly believe my ears. Shadow with a puppy. Who would take her for walks? Who would feed her at a civilized time? Who would let her out for her pees and poohs? And even worse, who would let her back inside once she had been relegated to the scrap-yard where she would be exposed to the elements in all their fury the way Popsie Miranda and I had been while Ma, the *boys* and Joyce had been in Egypt? No. I couldn't stand by silently and tolerate such an outrage. So I started to bark out my disapproval – and mark you, I said bark, not yap. Ma, whose command of Doglish was stupefyingly limited at times, completely failed to comprehend .what I was saying. The more I barked out my warning that Shadow would not take good or even reasonable care of Minette, Citoyenne de France, the more excitedly Ma responded, telling me with ever-increasing jubilance how pleased she was that I was pleased, when I was anything but. In desperation, I ran upstairs to the bedroom to fetch Popsie Miranda so that she could chorus her disapproval with mine. Notwithstanding that we went downstairs and stood directly in front of Ma, and barked and barked and barked for what seemed an eternity but must have been at the very least ten good minutes, she still failed to take on board what we were trying so desperately to communicate. I cannot tell you how frustrating it was to have our every bark met with cheerful pronouncements of delight on Ma's part. "How wonderful it is that you're so thrilled," was only one of the wildly inappropriate comments Ma kept on issuing, intermingled with others such as "Yes, I can see that you're overjoyed," and "How wonderful it is that you're so happy." Only when she said, "I've never seen either of you like this before," did she connect even momentarily with what we were so desperate to convey. It was true: We had never been like that before. But then, we had never been in such a troubling situation before.

As things turned out, I needn't have worried, though worry I did. So too did Popsie Miranda and Maisie Carlotta. Indeed, the only time I was ever genuinely grief-stricken at parting from a puppy was when Shadow came to pick up Minette, Citoyenne de France. The prospect of the awful life she would have with that refrigerator so chilled me with foreboding that I actually tried to prevent Shadow from leaving the house with the puppy. I stood on the front stoop with Maisie Carlotta beside me blocking Shadow's access to the front steps. "Aren't they sweet?" our naïve Ma said as Shadow stood impassively. "They don't want to part with her. Don't worry, darlings," she said to us, bending down to stroke us. "Minette, Citoyenne de France isn't leaving our lives forever. You'll see lots and lots of her." Ma then straightened up just as Popsie Miranda joined us and she said to Shadow, "It's extraordinary. I've never known them to react like this. They must have become extremely attached to the puppy. If it wasn't you who was taking her; and I know that we'll see lots of her in the future; and you'll bring her down to stay in the country when we go down for weekends, I don't think I'd have the heart to go through with this handover."

Two weeks later, Shadow informed Ma that the young daughter of a neighbour had so fallen in love with the puppy that she had asked if she could keep it for the weekend. Two weeks after that, she let slip accidentally on purpose, her every pore oozing deception, that she was having difficulty getting the puppy back from the neighbour. According to her, the mother was saying that it would break the little girl's heart if she lost the puppy.

Popsie Miranda and I exchanged meaningful glances. Having experienced for ourselves the way Shadow really functioned, we didn't even need our heightened senses of smell and hearing to see past the miasma of hypocrisy to the reality of what had happened. We knew as surely as my name was Tum Tum and hers was Popsie Miranda that Shadow had taken home the puppy, got fed up with having to deal with it, and handed it on to the first taker.

Which is exactly what happened, as I discovered when I came to Pet Heaven and could see all sorts of things from the past that I had not been able to while I was earth-bound.

Not that I knew this at the time Shadow was spinning her yarn. "Don't worry; she's a real dog-lover, just like you. Minette is very happy and settled where she is. I'll arrange for you to get together as soon as possible," Shadow said to Ma, who she knew insisted on in-depth interviews with all prospective new homes. That palliated Ma, but I could tell, just by what I was smelling and hearing that Shadow would never carry through on her promise. And she never did.

Chapter Ten

Minette, Citoyenne de France, was not the first of the puppies to go. That was Roddy Van Der Linden. Cam and Rupert came one Thursday afternoon shortly after the boys had come back from school. Rupert had bowled in, tail wagging enthusiastically, and greeted Maisie. He then said hello to me and Popsie Miranda while the puppies crowded around their father to get a good sniff of him. It would be fair to say that chaos reigned for all of about five minutes until Ma shrieked, "Bickies in basket." As if by magic, all of us, puppies included, tore towards our respective baskets, leaving Rupert in splendid isolation in the middle of the room.

After Ma had doled out our biscuits, she picked up Roddy and handed him over to Cam. I could hardly believe my nose when both she and Ma started to cry, the former from joy, the latter from something more complex. Of course, I could relate to Ma's feelings. Saying good-bye to one's progeny for the duration of one's earthly existence wasn't ever an agreeable experience, not even when they were going to good homes. But once all the puppies had been re-housed and we were left with just Maud, there was a welcome return to the peace and order that were ordinary features in our household.

Although having litters is a great joy, it's amazing how chaotic puppies are by the time they are six weeks old. Frankly, it was a welcome relief to have only Maud to train. One puppy on its own is easy to handle, for the natural tendency of most puppies on their own is a willingness to learn from their superiors. One really has to do very little except allow the puppy to follow one around and pick up through example what it should be doing. Problems only arise when the adult doesn't set a good example, which, of course, meant that no problems arose, for the one thing I was a good example.

Because I was top-dog, the task of disciplining the others had always been primarily mine. Although no tyrant, I did have a good, strong character to match my voice. Indeed, Ma had by this time taken to calling me Her Galactic Majesty Tum Tum, Centre of the Universe. There was no irony in that nickname, simply the recognition that I was a crystalline personality with a powerful pair of lungs which I did not shy away from using. But, as Ma was the first to admit, there was nothing unattractive or aggressive in my conduct. I was loving and simply liked an orderly as well as a happy environment. So, confronted with the need to train Maud up to the standard of the others, I set about the task with as light but firm a touch as I had employed with Popsie Miranda and Maisie Carlotta.

While a puppy will inevitably cling to its mother in the first weeks of its life, as it gets older it takes its place in the hierarchy of the pack. For Maud, this meant position number four. As she developed, she

Maud pictured with Maisie when calm had returned to the household.

The happy triumvirate: Michael, Dmitri and Maud.

assumed her place in the most delightful way. She created favourite spaces for herself that more than satisfied her requirements, without ever encroaching upon our territory. Nor was house-training any more of a problem with her than it had been with her canine mother and grandmother. I can truthfully say that I never once witnessed Maud having an accident inside.

Maud's personality was a true delight. Without being simpering, she was so incredibly loving with us canines and her human family that Ma started to call her "the love machine". Whenever she felt that someone needed love, or she simply wanted to give it to you, she would shut her eyes; relax her face in a way that was reminiscent of Hollywood divas from the silent era employing their best bedroom expressions. She would gently approach you and offer you this face beaming with nothing but love, thereby relaying the message that she was there to love and love she would until you had had all the love you needed. If you resisted her overtures, she would gently stroke you with her paw until you became more receptive.

As Maud grew up, I came to the conclusion that I was incredibly lucky in my descendants and family life. I can truthfully say that Popsie

Miranda, Maisie Carlotta, Maud and I never exchanged a wry word between us. Never once did we have a fight or squabble, except on the one occasion Joyce put down three bones from the butcher instead of four. We might well have come to grief if Joyce had not come back into the kitchen and put down the fourth bone.

Not only did we four doggies get along well, but we also hugely enjoyed each other's company. We had really good times too with Dmitri and Michael, who were growing into big boys. They remained very loving towards us, often playing with us when they came home from school, though I am pleased to say they were beginning to outgrow the phase of riding us.

As for Ma, she remained the same old reliable, loving Ma.

That summer, Joyce's employment contract came to an end. Ma decided that now that the boys were in school all day (the year before they had been in kindergarten for only half a day) she would try them with an *au pair* instead of a nurse.

Talk about a big mistake. The first girl was a nineteen year old Slovak called Jana who ate nothing but potatoes and white grapes and did not know the meaning of shutting a cupboard door. When Ma told her that it was not possible for her to leave the cupboard doors open in the kitchen, she informed her that her mother always closed them for her, and proceeded to leave them open. This was a major bore for me as well as for Ma, because we had an eat-in kitchen and she was causing a major obstruction whose only remedy was for Ma to shut the doors every time she came into the room. I would not have minded had the cupboards in question stocked food, but since they only housed things like plates and pots and pans and cleaning fluids, the inconvenience wasn't even worthwhile. Indeed, it was mightily irritating, but we only had to put up with this unbelievable scenario for a week, for Ma told her five days into her employment that she would have to find another family to work for if she left one more door open even once. I could tell from the scornful look she gave Ma that she had no intention of changing her habits, so it came as no surprise to me when Ma telephoned the agency and told them to replace her with someone who was 'housetrained'.

The replacement was even worse, if such a thing were possible.

Her name was Alice and she was older: twenty two. She had worked in England for a year but had had to return home a few months ago when her placement came to an end. The Czech Republic not yet being a part of the European Union, *au pairs* could only work in England if they had the necessary papers provided by their employers. The agency told Ma that Alice loved England and, being older and more mature, would not cause the problems Jana had. On that basis, Ma provided the letter of invitation that would allow her to enter the country; paid for her airline ticket; sent money for her to take the necessary buses and trains from her home town to Prague, where she would catch a flight to Heathrow Airport; and even provided her with the telephone number of the car service she used so that she could come from the airport without having to take public transport. Ma also instructed her not to take a black cab, for they were twice the price.

I knew Alice would be trouble from the moment I saw her climbing the steps to our front door. She did not arrive by black or mini cab. No sooner did Ma open the door for her than she asked her to give her back the £60 she had had to pay the taxi driver. When Ma asked her how it was that the price was so high, when she had provided her with the number of our car service, she said that she hadn't been able to reach them so had had to take a black cab. I could tell that she was lying. Not only did her pores betray her with the stench of deceit, but her clothes were wreathed with the scent of the tube.

It was obvious that Ma was dubious, but, Ma being Ma, she decided to make the best of a bad deal and gave Alice the £60 before taking her downstairs to the bedroom she would have exclusive use of on the ground floor. "Make yourself at home. After you've settled in, I'll show you the ropes," Ma said, then left her downstairs while she headed upstairs to her desk.

I could hardly believe my eyes when, five minutes later, Alice tip-toed upstairs. She must have been a heck of a lot stronger than she looked, for she was lifting her heavy suitcase clear off the ground. Stealthily, she made her way towards the front door, taking care not to make a sound in case Ma heard her. I toyed with the idea for all of a second or two of yapping out a warning to Ma to let her know what was happening, but then thought better of it. There was nothing about this bright-eyed, over-confident girl that I liked. Let her make her escape. In so doing, she would provide us with ours. So I merely looked at her knowingly.

Half an hour later, when Ma had finished whatever it was she was doing, she went downstairs to speak to Alice, only to discover that she had absconded.

"If you live long enough, I suppose you will see everything," Ma said ruefully. She marched back upstairs and telephoned the agency. She told them what had happened and demanded that they return the £60 she had given Alice, as well as the cost of her plane, rail and bus tickets. They must have been pretty embarrassed, because they not only agreed to do so but offered to waive their fee for Alice's replacement.

Alice's replacement was another Alice who also came from the Czech Republic. Presumably, Lewis Carroll was as popular in the former Hapsburg Empire as he had been in England in Victoria's heyday, for I had yet to meet one Alice in England, yet here were back to back Czech Alices. Aside from the fantastical elements of the Wonderland, maybe there was also something in the waters of the Danube as it flowed through Prague that made Czech Alice as adept at chicanery as the Carrolian Alice had been at phantasmagoria.

This latest Alice appeared to be all sweetness and light. She seemed eager to work, especially when she discovered that we already had a housekeeper, who did all the heavy cleaning, my beloved Mackie whom I knew all my life and not only gave me lots of love but lots of treats too. All Alice needed to do was prepare breakfast for the *boys* and take them to school in the morning (Ma always picked them up in the afternoon); play with them in the late afternoon after they came back home from school; give them their supper (which Ma usually cooked); baby-sit them when Ma was out; and once a week wash their clothes and change their linen. Unless, of course, Ma was away, in which case she would also have to let us *girls* into the garden every four hours for us to do our business, and feed us twice a day. Hardly arduous work, I am sure you agree.

But Alice Mach 2 was resourceful. She had figured out that there was stuff worth stealing in the house. Rather than pilfer it bit by bit, which she – rightly as it turns out – surmised Ma would have noticed, she waited until Ma was abroad for a week promoting her latest book in America, to put her plan into motion.

I knew all about the plan, because Alice had been dumb enough to think she could make arrangements with her English boyfriend right in front of me and I wouldn't be able to understand. I, a born Scot, unable to comprehend basic English, while she, a Czech who mangled the language at every turn but nevertheless managed to make herself understood, could plot and scheme in my native tongue while everything went sailing over my head. I would show her.

Her come-uppance began on the Thursday morning after she returned from dropping the *boys* off at school. As she whizzed around the house, taking out various items she intended him to help himself to, I fetched Popsie Miranda, Maisie Carlotta and Maud. We followed her from room to room, never so closely that she would consider us a nuisance, but closely enough to observe what was going on.

When Alice had finished her preparations, she went downstairs to her bedroom, removed her handbag from the cupboard where she secreted it as if anyone would have wanted to steal it, and headed back upstairs to the upper ground floor at quite a clip, I can tell you. She was on the mobile telephone Ma had got for Joyce after Dmitri was nearly abducted saying, "I'm about to leave now. Give it ten minutes then come. I'll leave the front door on the latch so all you'll need to do is give it a little push. Just remember there are dogs but you don't need to be frightened of them. They're very tame and if you give them something to eat, they'll stand by wagging their tails as you clean out the place."

No sooner were those words out of Alice's mouth than she was out the door. Sure enough, she left it on the latch; despite having strict instructions from Ma that she must at all times double-lock the door whenever she was not at home.

Well, there was no way I was going to allow any crooked *au pair* to clean Ma out of her treasures. I delegated Maisie Carlotta and Maud to stand guard in the passage leading to the front door, while Popsie Miranda and I went for help.

Getting the door open was quite a challenge, I don't mind admitting. Because we couldn't reach the handle, I had to use my front paw to pry it open the way I used to with the fridge door when we lived at West Eaton Place. Even though Ma would never be aware of it, my 'naughtiness', as she used to term it, was being applied in a wholly noble way. That surely wiped out any offence I had committed all those years ago.

It took awhile to figure out that there were substantial differences between the Bourne Street front door and the fridge door at West Eaton Place, but once I had done so, I realized that the way to strike pay dirt was to wedge my nails between the door and the frame then yank them back suddenly. That should spring the door. Which, sure enough, it did, though it took about seven or eight tries before the opening was wide enough for me to get my foot in place to yank open the door fully.

Once I had done so, things started to fall into place. I motioned Popsie Miranda to follow me. As I crossed our stoop and hopped down the five steps to the pavement at street level, she was shadowing me so closely that I could feel her breath on my back thigh.

At street level, I had to figure out how best to foil Alice's damnable scheme. I yapped at one or two passers-by, but they rather stupidly

I start down the front stoop with Popsie Miranda beside me.

thought that we were waiting for our master or mistress. As if any dog-lover would leave their pet to perambulate on Bourne Street in Belgravia. I tell you, it was at times like those that one realized how taxing being a dog on earth could be.

Popsie Miranda wouldn't have been Popsie Miranda if she didn't come up with a solution that was both elegant and restful. When she had had quite enough of everyone coming and going and misunderstanding our predicament, she turned tail with her usual grace and hopped back up the steps in a bluster of waggling skirts. She then surveyed the scene, easing herself down near our front door, and draped her right front paw decorously over the boot-brace that had been built with the house in the early days of Queen Victoria's reign in the 1830s. So gracious and serene did she look that any observer would have thought that Ma allowed her to take the afternoon air on the stoop.

I knew, however, that looks are deceptive. Popsie Miranda might have appeared to be serene, but she was also vigilant, and if anyone approached her, she would defend her turf with a ferocity they would find astonishing.

Relieved that the only access point to our house was covered by my pulchritudinous daughter, but frustrated that no one was assisting us, I suddenly had a brainwave. I would go to Susan, our next-door

Popsie Miranda and Maud (with me in the background) re-enact for Ma how we saved the day.

neighbour at number 44, and knock on her door.

Once in front of her door, however, I realized that I had nothing to knock with. Nor was I tall enough to ring her doorbell. Ruing the fact that I had never attained my old golden-retriever companion Nosher's height, I tried banging against the door with my body, but quickly saw that this would get me nowhere.

What to do? What to do? Unless I was quick, Alice's English boyfriend would arrive on the scene and then we'd have another whole set of problems to contend with. So I did what any sensible dog would do. I started to howl as loudly and continuously as I could.

Ma, of course, had always said that I had a voice that would wake the dead. Would this turn out to be true? Susan, I knew, was at home. I could smell her downstairs in the kitchen. She had the most delightfully fragrant scent, a combination of expensive French *parfum* and loving kindness. But would the famous Tum Tum voice be loud enough to reach her ears?

The answer to my question, I discovered soon enough, was a resounding yes. A panicked Susan ran up the stairs wondering what on earth was causing this cacophony. She opened her door with a flourish, her flushed cheeks glowing pink in the September sun. "My goodness Tum Tum, what on earth is the matter with you? And why are you here and not at home?" she asked, knowing very well that I had no business being anywhere but safely tucked up at home behind closed doors.

Ma and Susan had an arrangement whereby, whenever one of them was away, the other always looked out for any unusual activity in the adjoining house.

"Wait right there," she instructed me. "I'll just run and get the house keys." I supposed she meant both hers and ours, for she had both. She didn't even need to tell me that she planned to take me back home. Or that she would be demanding an explanation of the *au pair* and filing a full report with Ma as soon as her plane touched down at Heathrow. This was activity of the most unusual sort, just the type of thing that she and Ma had been guarding against since we had moved into the house a year and a half previously.

No sooner did Susan return and lock her door than her face fell almost to the street when she saw Popsie Miranda ensconced on the stoop. "What on earth is going on?" she asked rhetorically as she approached my lovely Popsie and gave her an affectionate rustle of the tufts sticking out of her forehead.

You might well ask, I wanted to say, but of course, I had no English and Susan had no Doglish, so we just had to muck in as best we could, with yaps and licks and wagging tails and lots of licks and even a springing up or two onto her skirt now that Ma wasn't around to reprimand us.

Susan was just about to ring the doorbell when Alice's boyfriend arrived on the scene. He hadn't been expecting anyone to be there, so he paused, a look of absolute disbelief on his face. Gathering up his wits, he seemed to decide that he must have the wrong house number, or that he had confused our house with Susan's, for he then committed the cardinal error of walking past ours to Susan's. In two steps he had bounded up her stoop and was standing before her front door. She didn't even have a chance to say anything before he was trying to push her door open.

"Can I help you?" she asked as he turned to her, a look of complete befuddlement wreathing his face.

"I'm looking for Alice," he said.

"Alice doesn't work at my house. She works here," Susan said.

"Tell her I'll be in touch," he said, and started to retreat down the steps. The expression on his face could not have stated more clearly that his plans had gone profoundly awry.

"Who shall I say left the message?" Susan asked in all innocence.

"It doesn't matter. She'll know," he said shiftily, as he bounded down the steps and ran off in the direction of Graham Terrace, where he had parked his van preparatory to carting off the haul.

The penny still hadn't dropped for Susan. It did only after she had rung the doorbell of our house and, when no one answered, she noticed that the front door was not closed. Pushing it open, she was confronted by Maisie Carlotta and Maud sitting guard in the passage. Behind them were several piles of stuff which Alice had left out for her boyfriend to take.

Susan entered the house, closely followed by Popsie Miranda and me. Of course, Maisie Carlotta and Maud greeted her with all the warmth they reserved for particular favourites. As she stroked my descendents, she called out for Dmitri, Michael and Alice. No one, of course, was in. It was only when she saw this that she began to discern that something sinister was afoot. "I wonder if this was a put-up job," Susan said as she went in search of Ma's number to telephone her and alert her to these strange happenings.

Having located the number, she rang Ma. They agreed that the whole thing was deeply suspicious. But with Ma away, discretion was the better part of valour. To let Alice know that they had seen through her ploy would be to beg for further trouble. So Susan stayed with us until Alice returned home with the *boys*.

Any doubts that Susan might have had about Alice's role in things was immediately removed when our benevolent neighbour saw our conniving *au pair's* expression as she opened up the door and saw Susan in the sitting room, surrounded by all the items she had left out for her boyfriend to steal. But Susan was cleverer and more circumspect than this Danubian devil. She acted as if nothing was amiss although one glimpse of the waiting haul had been all it took for her to get the whole picture.

After greeting Dmitri and Michael with the fondness she always showed them, Susan said, "You need to make sure that the front door is double-locked every time you go out. Someone seems to have managed to get it open and Tum Tum and Popsie Miranda were in the street. You can imagine how awful it would have been if they had come to any harm. You will be more careful in the future, won't you?"

"Oh yes," a crestfallen Alice said. "I will be sure to be more careful in future."

As soon as Susan left, Alice stuck the *boys* in front of the television, and while they were watching cartoons, she packed back the things she had taken out for removal. Later, I overheard her speaking to her boyfriend on the telephone. They were rescheduling the burglary for Ma's next visit abroad, whenever that might be. But they never got the opportunity to enact their plan, for, as soon as Ma returned from New

York, she told Alice that she could have two weeks wages and leave immediately, or she could face a police investigation. Naturally, Alice took the money and ran.

And I basked in Ma's approbation yet again as she once more flooded us all with so many chews and treats that even my jaw started to give out under the strain of so much mastication.

At this juncture, I was not the only member of the family in luck. Ma too hit a good spell when our next *au pair* arrived from Croatia. Arianna was a Greek and Latin scholar whose great-uncle had been the famous Cardinal Stepinac who used to bless the troops in the Second World War from behind a vast cross. You can imagine how unpopular his family was under the Communists, but by the time Arianna came to stay with us, Croatia was no longer Communist and her family was on the upswing after four decades of revilement. Having seen the best and worst of humanity against a backdrop of intelligence and education, Arianna had a sound, solid, sensitive character. She was kind, civilized, decent and loving. She was particularly fond of kids and dogs, which was all Ma ever required of anyone to think that they were the best thing since sliced bread, and within a matter of weeks the *boys* and us *girls* were as fond of her as Ma was.

That Christmas, Ma sent Arianna back to Croatia for the holidays. The rest of us decamped to Haresfield, which turned out to be the ideal

We all lucked out when Arianna joined our household.

place to be, especially after we had a series of snowfalls which buried the whole area in a deep layer of white.

When the *boys* were not playing with Amy and us *girls*, they could be found at Vickie's house where they spent hours playing with her and Anna. Oliver remained as big a wuss as ever, and could be relied upon to flee behind Mama Vickie's skirts at all times. Sometimes Ma would let the *boys* take us *girls* with them to Vickie's. This was always fun, especially when we were outside in the snow, though I have to admit that Oliver was no more courageous with us than he was with our human brothers. Loving, yes. Sweet, yes. But oh what a nervous Nellie.

One morning after a particularly heavy snowfall, Vickie rang Ma to ask her if she would join her, Anna and Oliver for a tobogganing session with the *boys* and us *girls*. Vickie proposed that we all walk up to the top of Haresfield Beacon (something we often did with Vickie, Anna and Oliver, though seldom with Ma, who was averse to too much physical exertion). I wasn't surprised when Ma begged off but allowed the rest of us to go. Had she known what was about to happen, there is no way she would have behaved as she did.

Dmitri and Michael had rather large and snazzy looking red toboggans. After Ma had dressed them in their snug snowsuits, she waved them off, watching laughingly as they dragged these through the snow to Vickie's house, with Popsie Miranda, Maisie Carlotta, Maud and me following in their wake.

After linking up with Anna, Vickie and Oliver, who had two somewhat smaller but equally effective toboggans, we set off towards the main gate. Across from it was a railroad siding. Beyond that were the train tracks where the Gloucester to London express train ran. The boys used to love to watch the trains speed past, but that was not a pastime I found particularly pleasurable. The roar of the train as it flew by was too unnerving for my – or indeed any dogs' – liking, but fortunately there was no chance of a train running on that morning, for the 'wrong' sort of snow had fallen and all train services had been cancelled.

After crossing the train tracks, we all set off up the hill towards the Beacon. There was so much snow that balls kept on forming between my paws, but I didn't let that bother me as we trudged joyously up the slopes until we reached the top of the Beacon.

Vickie and Anna had brought a basket of refreshments with them, so, after selecting the ideal spot for it, they put it down, settled us five doggies around it, then started the fun and games of tobogganing down the road, which the snow had turned into the perfect run.

Although I knew better than to try to open the basket, my nostrils were being assailed by the most delicious scents. Without even having to look, I knew that Anna had prepared a large thermos of hot chocolate as well as croissants and other delectables for when they and the *boys* got peckish. And because Vickie and Anna were dog lovers, there were treats reposing there for Oliver and us *girls* too.

Although I was enjoying being out and about, there came a point when sitting quietly beside the fragrant basket became too much of temptation. So I started sniffing it, hoping to find a weak spot which I could utilize to pry it open and take out my treat. There was never any intention on my part to eat Vickie and Anna's or the *boys'* snacks, the other doggie treats, but once I had managed to get the lid to flip open, temptation got the better of me. I was just about to tuck into some croissants and Orange Marmalade when I heard Vickie booming, "Stop that, Tum Tum. I can see you."

Oh my gosh, I thought as I froze to the spot. Caught red handed. I raised my head and was about to yap out an apology when Vickie started to laugh. "You are incorrigible Tum Tum. I knew it would be too much to expect you to leave that basket alone. Come here."

Chastened but relieved to see that Vickie harboured no ill-feelings, I ran over to her just as she took a biscuit out of her pocket and gave it to me. Once I had wolfed it down, she said, "You'd better come toboggan with us."

"I'll take Tum Tum," Michael said. "She can ride with me."

"Then I want Popsie Miranda," Dmitri said.

"Fine, fine," Vickie laughed. "As long as they don't topple you over."

The first few runs were not exactly studies in stability, but by the fifth time, Popsie Miranda and I and the *boys* had all got the hang of how to keep our balance and whiz down the hillside without falling over. This was great fun, I don't mind telling you. All the more so for being so unexpected. I didn't know any other dogs who went tobogganing with their human siblings and neighbours. And to think we were not only doing it, but doing it well too.

After too short a time for my taste, Vickie said she had to return home. This cannot have been more than an hour after we had broken to have a snack, but she promised us more of the same the following day if conditions allowed.

Fortunately, conditions did allow. There had been another heavy snowfall the night before, so we had a welcome repeat of the day before. This time, we stayed out for even longer. Only when the *boys* were almost frozen solid did Vickie feel compelled to call a halt to the fun. Naturally, this evinced howls of protest from both of them. To placate them, Vickie promised them one last ride down the hill.

Lining up our various toboggans, Anna, Vickie, Dmitri, Michael, Popsie Miranda and I took our places. "On your marks. Get set. Go," Vickie bellowed as we shot off down the side of the Beacon. Oh, the joy, the indescribable delight as the trees on either side of the road whizzed past us. Michael and I were comfortably intertwined when I sensed, as only an animal can, that something was going dramatically wrong. I could tell that it wasn't a tsunami, or an earthquake, or anything as fundamentally earth shattering as that. But I could also tell that the effect would be equally disastrous for us if I did not intervene. So I did what any sensible dog would do. I toppled Michael and myself off the toboggan as it hurtled straight off the road into a huge boulder on the roadside.

Vickie, who had been behind us looking at where we were headed in horror, jumped off her toboggan and ran over to us. She plucked Michael out of the snow just as he said, "Tum Tum toppled me."

"Yes, darling. She did. And a good thing too, otherwise you might have injured yourself very badly."

"So Tum Tum was being good, then?" Michael enquired, not at all certain that I was due the praise I seemed to be getting.

"That she definitely was. I'll have to tell your mother so she can get you all the treats you deserve. Good old Tum Tum. Saving the day yet again."

Chapter Eleven

For the rest of 1997, I remained the picture of indestructibility that I had always been. But the New Year was the last time I would ever possess the robust good health I had enjoyed all my life (one can't count accidents as ill health, not when one has such a strong constitution that one weathers them with the alacrity that I had displayed in coping with mine).

As 1998 unfolded, it began to become apparent that I was no longer the fit, indomitable Tum Tum who had bounced back from my car accident with the vigour that I did. Although I remained as constitutionally strong as ever, with an appetite and bark that still had Ma in thrall to them, the damage done to my hind-quarters, when I was run down aged nine months by that car, started to kick in pretty smartly as I approached my thirteenth birthday.

At first, I resisted the decline to my mobility as best I could. When I could no longer run, I walked as fast as I could. Gradually, however, even walking became a struggle. Ma and I were in accord with how to cope with the problem. Having taken the best medical advice, we would soldier on for as long as I could.

And soldier on I did. When we went for walks in the park in London or in the fields in the country, I would linger with Ma and Popsie Miranda, who had long since stopped running, and now always walked beside Ma.

Here I am on the floor with Popsie Miranda chairing it and Maisie behind us on New Year's Day 1998.

The effects of my accident became more noticeable as I aged.

Then one day I found myself unable to keep up with them. This was definitely a step in the wrong direction, but Ma coped with it the way she had coped with so much else. She accommodated me by slackening her pace.

Although I could still walk up and down stairs, one night when we were all going up to bed in London, my back legs gave way beneath me. Ma helped me to get up and I managed to make it upstairs on that occasion, but within weeks I could no longer either climb up or down stairs. No matter how often I tried – and I can assure you, try I did, especially when Ma wasn't looking – every time I positioned myself on the stairs I would topple over and fall down them. So Ma started to lift me.

At first, she didn't realize that doing so was the equivalent of pressing weights in the gym, or that she would be developing muscles which she would prefer to remain undeveloped. To her credit, even when she realized that her shoulders were "starting to look like Madonna's", as she put it, she did not hesitate to gladly continue lifting me. For her, this was a labour of love, and though she felt that she was disfiguring her neck and shoulder line, she told me that she regarded this was a price well worth paying to have me with her still.

Ma took this photo of me just before climbing stairs became impossible.

It's just as well Ma had that attitude, for it was only a matter of a month or two after my back legs ceased to support me climbing up and down stairs when they failed in another major way. Whenever I toppled over, as I did more and more, it became increasingly difficult to get back on my feet. Then came the dreaded day when no matter how hard I tried to hoist myself up onto all fours, my wretched back legs simply would not function. I cannot convey how stupefied I was or how helpless and frustrated I felt the first time this happened. To make matters worse, Ma was out, the *boys* were upstairs in their bedroom with their nanny (Ma having given up on *au pairs* after Arianna had to return to Croatia), and I was two floors beneath them in the kitchen. So I started to bark and bark and bark, and I continued until they realized that something was wrong and came down to help me get back onto my feet.

On that occasion, Dmitri and Michael hoisted me up without any trouble and, after an initial degree of unsteadiness; I was firmly back on my four feet. Not for long, however. The next time I sat down, it proved as impossible for me to get up as it had been the last time.

As you can see, though I could no longer walk I was still fit and certainly enjoyed life, especially when I was in the kitchen soaking up the sun and looking through the window at the passing parade on the street.

Now I wasn't only frustrated, but frightened as well. Were my back legs condemning me – active me – to a life of immobility?

The answer, I fear, was yes. But Ma wasn't any more willing than I was to accept my predicament without doing what she could to alleviate it. Like me, she had a no-nonsense aspect to her personality, and once the new vet in London and John in the country told her there was nothing science could do to reverse the muscular degeneration which was a combination of the damage that had been done to my hind quarters all those years ago and old age, she told me that we would either have to learn to live with my paralysis or then I would have to be put down.

"If you were a human being, no one would consider killing you just because you can't walk, and I certainly don't intend to deprive you of your life because you're disabled. As far as I'm concerned, you and I have a sacred contract. It is my responsibility as well as great pleasure to take care of you – the best care of you I can manage – until your life comes to a natural end. Life is never perfect, and you certainly haven't lost your lust for life, so, my darling Tum, we'll just have to make the best of a bad deal and do everything in our power to keep you comfortable and enhance whatever quality remains in your life."

Ma, of course, was absolutely right. I had not lost my love of life. I still enjoyed my family, both canine and human. I still enjoyed my food. And I definitely enjoyed being out and about. It was a real relief to hear that my life wasn't coming to a premature end.

Ma was as good as her word. She coped with my paralysis as sensibly and with as little fuss as I had seen her cope with many of the other vicissitudes in her life, not the least of which was when Michael had been knocked down by a car at the age of three right in front of us.

Ma cut up old bath towels and made rigging to support my hind quarters so that I could pooh and pee standing up the way all doggies normally do. Of course, if you are paralysed you are more prone to weakness of the bladder, so she ensured that I was taken out so regularly for piddles that my skirts remained as dry as if I did not have a problem. She washed my hind quarters frequently and towel- and blow-dried them afterwards so that I wouldn't invite infection or bed sores as a result of dampness. So that my front legs wouldn't waste away through lack of exercise, she also took me for walks using the rigging to support my back legs, hunching over me even though this put a strain on her back. She even made enquiries about ordering the doggie equivalent of callipers, though she came to the conclusion that the benefits of such a contraption were illusory rather than real. Most importantly for someone as sociable as me, she made sure that I was never isolated the way so many paraplegics are. She took me everywhere I would have walked had I still been able to do so. The result was that she spent a good proportion of the day lifting me up and down stairs.

If the family was downstairs having dinner, I was right beside them the way I had always been. When the action shifted upstairs to the sitting room after dinner, I was duly transported there by Ma, who often as not made me walk to and from the stairs with the assistance of my rigging. Knowing how much I loved being out and about, she would even take me for drives in the car with her, settling me comfortably in the front passenger seat which had always been my favourite spot, so to that extent I was deriving a benefit the younger dogs seldom enjoyed and Popsie Miranda and I had ceased to once the *boys'* nurses came on the scene and could babysit us.

Best of all, I still accompanied the rest of the family for some of our daily constitutional in the park whenever we were in London, or in the grounds at Haresfield in the country. Of course, my walks were curtailed versions of theirs. Ma could hardly be expected to bend over me holding the rigging for the full duration of a normal walk, but she always ensured that I had a good two or three hundred years exercise each morning, before she settled me down comfortably in a spot where I could see and be seen until they returned.

At first, Ma had been reluctant to let me out of her sight in the park in London. She was worried about dognappers, but with the passage of time so many of the regular dog owners in Battersea Park offered to keep an eye on me while she was out of view, that we relaxed into an agreeable routine.

This lasted for several months until one day a hideous looking old crone, her face twisted with bitterness, came up to me, inspected my

Here I am enjoying the air in Battersea park.

collar, saw Ma's surname and telephone number with the distinctive Belgravia prefix of 730, muttered about how dreadful it was that posh people felt they could do anything they wanted with humans and animals, and announced that she intended to "teach the cow a lesson" for leaving me unattended.

Normally, I responded to the overtures of strangers openly, but there was something so dark and oppressive about the way this woman was behaving, that I recoiled from her attentions. I tried as best I could to wriggle away from her as she bent down and tried to pick me up, but when she grabbed me forcibly by my shoulders, I started to howl in protest. This brought over Stephanie, a lovely, elegant and mature lady who had had polio as a child and walked with a limp and a gold-topped stick. "That's Tum Tum," she said in an attempt to break up this misadventure. "She's here every morning. We all know her and keep an eye on her for her owner, whom I know. She's quite all right, I can assure you."

"This dog has been abandoned," the crone said angrily. "Any dog that's left on its own by its owner has been abandoned."

"She hasn't. She's paralyzed. But she loves coming to the park. I know her very well. She always yaps out a greeting to everyone she knows. And quite a few she doesn't. Don't you Tum Tum?" she said, bending down to stroke me and get her daily lick.

"You are as bad as the owner. Covering up dog abuse. This dog has been abandoned and it is my duty to rescue her."

"I can assure you neither I nor her owner is abusing her. Please leave well alone."

"Disgraceful," the crone spat, and before I could swivel my head round, she had gathered me up in her arms and was carrying me to her car while I was protesting both orally and with wriggles. "This dog belongs at the Battersea Dogs' Home. If she does have an owner, you can tell her that's where I have taken her. Cow."

Just as this creature, who would not have been amiss swearing oaths over the cauldron in Macbeth, was struggling to open her car door, I saw Ma turn the corner in the distance. One didn't need a particularly active imagination to envisage how appalled she would be not to see me in my customary spot. Intent on capturing her attention, I started to bark as loudly as I could, but she didn't hear me, though I did see her speaking to Stephanie as the crone dumped me unceremoniously and forcefully in the bask seat of her dirty vehicle.

That witch didn't have time to drop me off and depart from Battersea Dogs Home before Ma burst into the reception area, urgently saying, "Someone has kidnapped my dog and brought her here. Her name is Tum Tum and she is crippled. Do you have her?"

"She has not been kidnapped. She has been rescued," the crone turned and informed Ma triumphantly, pushing her face into Ma's as she did so.

While she was doing so, one of the attendants said, "She's right here." Ma looked, saw me sitting comfortably by the admissions' desk, turned to the crone, and said, "Get your face out of mine, you filthy, interfering troublemaker. Stephanie told you Tum Tum was perfectly okay. What perverse satisfaction can you get from causing trouble for people and innocent animals? Your assertion that I abandoned Tum Tum is defamatory and I invite you to withdraw it or provide me with your name and address so that my lawyer can issue proceedings for slander against you."

I was amused by how quickly the crone shot out of the Dogs' Home once she realized that Ma wasn't a pushover. But Ma wasn't going to let her off so lightly. She followed her outside and I could hear her remonstrating with her and demanding her name and address, which the woman continued refusing to give. I could tell that Ma was winding the encounter up and would soon be back inside for me when she said, "You are not only a mischief maker but a coward. I am going to provide the (Battersea Dogs') Home with my contact details so that they can get in touch with me should you pull a stunt like this at anyone else's expense. If you do, I will add my nail to your coffin and make sure you're buried under the dross that you are."

Seconds later, Ma was back inside. The staff did their best to calm her down, telling her how obvious it was that I had not been abandoned – not only was I a picture of good health, my paralysis aside, but our contact details were engraved on a silver disc on my collar – and they had intended to telephone her as soon as the dognapper had left. But Ma was so agitated and angry that she kept on repeating, "I simply don't understand how anyone can be so wicked," while she simultaneously thanked them for their concern and gathered me up in her arms to take me back home.

If this upset was uncalled for, it was minor compared with what lay in store for all of us a few weeks later. It was April 2000. Ma had taken the boys skiing in Klosters in Switzerland. Thelma, the nurse who had taken over from Arianna was taking care of us, and good care it was too. Unlike Joyce, who was basically indifferent to animals though not unkind, or Jennifer, who really despised animals, she was one of those Jamaican country folk who actually like dogs. She enjoyed us sitting with her as much as we did, and often, when Ma was out or away, all five of us would sit curled up on her bed looking at television.

The four of us *girls* were doing exactly that when Popsie Miranda coughed. And coughed. And coughed again. She slithered off the bed onto the floor. She coughed one more time. The room filled with the pungent odour of blood as Thelma and I looked down at the blob of red matter on the carpet which she had just expectorated. "Popsie Miranda, what is that?" Thelma, who had a diploma in medical nursing as opposed to nannying, said in a tone of voice that was so laden with concern that all of us immediately knew that something was seriously amiss. Popsie Miranda looked up at Thelma with a wan expression, as if to say, "I don't know what's happening." And Thelma, bless her soul, understood.

"I'd better take you to the vet," Thelma said, and without even stopping to telephone ahead to make an appointment, got Popsie Miranda's lead, put it on and was out of the door on their way to the Elizabeth Street. Veterinary Clinic three blocks away.

At the clinic, the duty vet diagnosed pneumonia and suggested that Thelma leave Popsie Miranda overnight. As soon as she came back home, she telephoned Ma to break the news to her. I could hear Ma saying, "I don't like the sound of this. I'll phone the vet right now." Ten minutes later, Ma telephoned Thelma again. "They say it's pneumonia but they think they can get it under control with antibiotics and there's no need for me to return home early." Ma was due back in two days time in any event.

The following afternoon Thelma rang Ma again to tell her that the vet had said she could come and pick Popsie Miranda up, as her condition had improved. "That's certainly a relief," Ma said. "I was so worried I didn't get a wink of sleep last night."

There was never any doubt in my mind or Popsie Miranda's that Ma was utterly devoted to us, so it came as no surprise when she returned from the trip with an odour of such anxiety that my heart went out to her. Although Popsie Miranda was clearly not fit, her breathing was less laboured than it had been, and she was on antibiotics, so Ma's pores started giving off the fragrance of relief once she saw her, though I could sense she would remain on edge until Popsie Miranda was fully recovered.

For a day or two, Popsie Miranda's condition remained stable. Ma being Ma, she took her to the vet every day for a check up, saying, "The one thing we all need is our lungs. I prefer to err on the side of caution than to leave the door open for trouble."

This was one time, however, that no amount of care could keep trouble away. Despite appearances, Popsie Miranda was not getting any better.

That Friday evening, we were happily hurtling down the M5, heading for Haresfield in anticipation of a cosy weekend with our houseguest Mangal, of whom we were all fond, when Popsie Miranda, who was sitting at his feet, started to gasp for air.

"Oh my God, Popsie Miranda. Don't tell me your pneumonia's

back," Ma said with such dread in her voice that I could tell she felt our beloved daughter's life was in danger.

No sooner were the words out of her mouth than she jammed her foot on the accelerator with such force that the car shot off likes a bullet. She tore down the motorway while Mangal held Popsie Miranda in his lap, stroking her in an attempt to relax my distressed daughter, until we came to the Stonehouse bypass. Burning rubber, Ma screeched around the corner in a mean imitation of Michael Schumacher in a Formula 1 race. She kept her foot on the floorboard until we reached the house in record time. By then, the crisis had passed. Popsie Miranda's breathing was once more relatively normal, but this was only a partial relief for Ma. She took her in her arms, ran into the house with her, shouting to Mangal and Thelma to unload the car and take care of all of us while she telephoned John, our country vet.

By the time we had done our business and been taken inside by Mangal and Thelma, Ma was winding up her conversation with John. "He says, of what I've told him, there's no need to bring her in tonight, but he'd like to see her first thing tomorrow. So we'll take her in at nine o'clock, if you don't mind the early rise," she said to Mangal.

At the appointed hour the following morning, we all poured into the car and headed for John's surgery in the nearby town of Quedgley. As soon as we pulled up in the parking lot, I got ready to hop out. There was no way I was going to allow Ma to leave me behind. Not when I wanted to hear, see and smell for myself exactly what was going on, canine senses being far more penetrating and reliable than human. After all, Popsie Miranda was not only by daughter, but also my beloved companion, and there was no way I intended to rely solely upon Ma conveying the information John would impart to her when I could assess it for myself. So I tried to leap out of the car as soon as she opened the door, only to collapse in a heap on the asphalt. Ma stood to one side while she gently held back Maisie Carlotta and Maud and let Popsie Miranda out.

"Isn't that sweet?" Mangal observed. "Tum Tum wants to go with Popsie Miranda."

"And so she shall," Ma said as she bent down, picked me up, and took me in with Popsie Miranda and Mangal.

We can't have been waiting in the reception area for more than five minutes before John came out to escort us into the examination room. Before we even reached the room, Ma was telling him what the new vet at Elizabeth Street had told her about Popsie Miranda's condition.

"I don't like the symptom of coughing up blood. That's not a feature of pneumonia," he said as he heaved Popsie Miranda up onto the examination table.

He took out his stethoscope and listened to her chest. He examined her gums and looked at Ma with a sad expression. "I hate to say this, but this dog is critical."

"Critical, what do you mean: critical?" Ma said; panic oozing from her voice and pores.

"Critical," he said quietly, at which Ma burst into tears and started to babble about how healthy-looking Popsie Miranda's stool had been no more than an hour ago.

"If it's not pneumonia, what do you think it is?" Mangal said. We could all tell he was trying to help.

"There are one or two alternatives, neither very good news, I'm afraid."

"Such as," Ma croaked between her tear-filled gasps.

"Well," John said, obviously hating having to convey such distressing facts, "the first thing that comes to mind is............" long pause, then very quietly, "tuberculosis."

"Tuberculosis," Ma repeated, so shocked that I feared she would collapse.

"There are other alternatives," John said gently. "But no matter what the problem turns out to be, you must steel yourself for the fact that she is critical."

"What do you recommend?" Ma wanted to know as Popsie Miranda and I looked at each other, pitying her more than one another. She had flooded the room with such odours of distress that we were amazed that neither John nor Mangal was hugging her. So I started to yap consolingly while Popsie Miranda licked her hand.

"Since Elizabeth Street has been treating her and you have to be in London during the week, I'd suggest you take her back tomorrow evening and let them continue," he said.

On the way back to Haresfield I could tell that Ma had not absorbed the severity of John's message. She still smelt of hopefulness, which in a way was understandable, as no one wants to lose a loved one, even if it is only for the blink of an eyelid in eternal terms. And

The weather was so good that Ma made Popsie Miranda take the air on Sunday.

Despite her optimism, Ma took photos of the four of us together-just in case.

Ma, being a human being, had the double disadvantage of not only loving us passionately but also of having an insufficiently canine attitude to separation.

For the remainder of the weekend, Ma sought refuge in the possibility that John might be wrong. She watched Popsie Miranda like a hawk, and took comfort from the fact that she had no more 'turns' the way she had done in the car.

Bright and early on Monday morning she and Popsie Miranda were back at Elizabeth Street. Once more they held out hope. Needless to say, Ma clutched at it, but at four o'clock on the Tuesday morning Popsie Miranda had another turn. Ma was so frightened she could barely talk as she arranged to take our beloved daughter back in to Elizabeth Street for her to be put into the canine equivalent of an oxygen tent.

At lunchtime Ma telephoned for an update. "If she were a human being, she would be in intensive care," the vet told Ma.

"Then put her in it," Ma said.

"We don't have the facilities here. The only place that does is the Royal Veterinary College in Potters Bar." This was an hour away from London. Ma knew it well because her mother-in-law's best friend lived nearby and she used to go to Sunday lunch there from time to time.

"Make the arrangements," Ma said, and rushed upstairs to change out of her writing clothes into something more appropriate.

I dearly wanted to go with them, and kept on yapping out my request from my vantage point in the sitting room. But Ma was so frantic I could tell there was no way she would take me, and sure enough, as she was leaving, she said, "I'm sorry, Tum Tum. I know you want to come. But not this time, honey."

I did not need to be there to know what happened next, for Ma gave all of us such a detailed account during the following days that I could see it in my mind's eye as if I had indeed been there. After she collected Popsie Miranda, who remained rigged up to drip her, from Elizabeth Street, she drove as fast as she could to the Royal Veterinary College, where they were awaiting them. When she arrived, one of the nurses helped her into reception with Popsie Miranda, whom she kept on her lap, stroking her gently, until the vet came out to see them.

He took one look at Popsie Miranda and said, "You have to say goodbye. We have no time to spare. We have to get her into the operating theatre right now."

"Say goodbye? I'm coming," Ma said.

"You can't come. You have to say goodbye. Right now. She's dying and we might not be able to save her."

So far, no one had actually mentioned death, but now that this vet had done so, Ma could no longer take refuge in false hope. She promptly burst into tears. But this time, she was so upset that she was sobbing uncontrollably. She hugged Popsie Miranda and said, "Popsie Miranda darling, I love you so much. Thank you for all the joy you've brought us all." She kissed Popsie Miranda on the side of her face, stroked the cute wisp of curls on her forehead, and ran her hand over her side as the vet lifted her up off her lap into his arms. A second later, he was running in the direction of the operating theatre while one of the nurses stood beside a sobbing Ma stroking her arm consolingly.

Forty five minutes later, the vet came back outside and said he needed to see Ma privately. He waited until they were seated in his office before saying, "Popsie Miranda is terminal. She has lung cancer. Her lungs are almost completely consolidated. She will be dead very shortly unless you put her down. I strongly recommend it."

"I can't," Ma said. "I could never live with myself if I was responsible for killing her. But I do believe in pain management, even if it shortens life. Is she in pain?"

"No, but we can give her something for any discomfort there might be."

"Please do that," Ma said. "Then I'll take her home for her to die surrounded by her loved ones. She will make it back home, won't she?"

"These things are always difficult to gauge, but I'd say she'll die later tonight or early tomorrow," he said.

Popsie Miranda told me she didn't know how Ma managed to drive them back home without crashing the car. All the way back to Belgravia, she was wracked with great, heaving sobs. She was so disconsolate she missed the Swiss Cottage turning and nearly ended up

*Popsie Miranda looking as fit as a fiddle in the sitting
room just before dinner.*

in the City, which of course added a good forty minutes to the journey.
This caused her to apologize to Popsie Miranda, but Popsie Miranda
didn't mind. Her head was in Ma's lap and, weak though she was, she
was enjoying all the strokes and love-talk Ma was giving her between
the sobs, especially as how the analgesic the vet had given her had taken
the edge off her discomfort in a most agreeable way.

Popsie Miranda and Ma arrived back home at about six o'clock.
Although Popsie Miranda could walk, Ma nevertheless brought her in,
in her arms. She laid her down on the sofa and, surrounded by the *boys*,
Thelma, and us *girls,* repeated what the vet had told her.

"You need to say goodbye to Popsie Miranda," Ma told Dmitri
and Michael. "You need to thank her for all the good things she's
brought into your life, and let her depart this life knowing you've
appreciated her love and that you love her."

I don't think either Dmitri or Michael really understood what Ma
was telling them. No one they knew or loved had ever died, at least not
since they were old enough to understand what was happening (their
uncle and grandfather had died when they were a year old). So they
told Popsie Miranda good-bye with levity, as if they expected her to be
around even after her death. Then they asked when supper was going
to be ready, stating that they were hungry.

While Thelma was dishing up supper, and Ma was preparing our bowls – Popsie Miranda's included – Aunt Kari telephoned. As soon as she heard the news, she offered to come and sit with Ma. She arrived after we had all eaten supper, even Popsie Miranda having managed to eat a little. Shadow also arrived, which none of us minded, for her presence would provide Ma with additional comfort, and it was clear to all of us that Ma would need all the comforting she could get.

The vigil now started in earnest. While Aunt Kari, Shadow and Ma sipped champagne and talked, I sat on the sofa beside Popsie Miranda, whose head was in Ma's lap. Occasionally she would shift position, sometimes sitting up for a short while, other times simply curling up beside Ma, before placing her head back in Ma's lap. Meanwhile, Aunt Kari, Shadow and Ma continued to sip champagne and talk quietly, the atmosphere laden with anticipation as the countdown to death continued.

When the clock struck eleven and Popsie Miranda was still with us, Ma took the four of us girls out for a quickie in the back garden. Although Popsie Miranda's breathing became slightly more laboured

Aunt Kari, Ma and I comfort Popsie Miranda and each other while Maisie looks on.

with the exertion, once she was back on the sofa with Ma, it returned to normal. "If you didn't know anything was wrong, you wouldn't be able to tell," Aunt Kari said, giving voice to what Ma was also thinking.

"I'm so glad she's so peaceful and comfortable," Ma said.

"You can tell she draws great comfort from being in her Mummy's arms," Aunt Kari said, voicing another truth.

"And I from having her in mine," Ma said, running her hand up and down Popsie Miranda's side as her voice caught tearfully.

At five minutes past midnight, we were all sitting peacefully when Popsie Miranda took a great big gasp, he body stiffened, she lay her head in Ma's lap, and was gone, all in the space of a few seconds.

"Thank God it was peaceful and quick," Ma said, breaking down into tears as she covered Popsie Miranda with kisses, and thanked her at the same time for having been such a wonderful daughter to her.

Maisie Carlotta and Maud, realizing what had happened, came over to tell Popsie Miranda good-bye. After they had done so, Ma shifted me into pole position so that I too could tell my beloved daughter and companion good-bye. When I had given her the last sniff and lick, Aunt Kari said she would open Ma's car, which was parked right outside the house, for her, while Ma lifted Popsie Miranda's inert body. Aunt Kari and Shadow then accompanied Ma to Elizabeth Street, where she said her final good-byes. Afterwards, they would cremate her and send Ma back the ashes, which she will one day have intermingled with her own as well as mine and all her other beloved pets so that we will be symbolically as well as actually together for all time.

Chapter Twelve

Popsie Miranda's death came as such a shock to Ma that it took her weeks to reconcile it with her expectations. She had truly believed that I would be the first to go to Pet Heaven, especially as how I had aged dramatically in the last year or so, while Popsie Miranda had not. She had looked the very picture of health when Ma had left for that skiing trip to Klosters, and indeed remained both healthy-looking and ravishingly beautiful until she drew her last breath. She had been a healthy weight. She had had a good appetite. Her digestive system had been in good shape every day Ma inspected our stool to make sure it reflected good health. She had looked far younger than the thirteen years less thirteen days she was when she left this earth. All the gauges Ma had utilized to check our health had been deceptive where Popsie Miranda was concerned, and now Ma, always vigilant of our welfare and that of the *boys*, had to come to terms with this unexpected loss.

Sometimes she would hug me and say tearfully, "Tum Tum, I only hope you don't miss Popsie Miranda as much as I do. I had no idea anything was wrong with her. If only I'd had a clue, maybe I could have done something to save her." I would yap out consoling sentiments which she understood and appreciated, though I did not try to communicate the intricacies of why she should treat death in a more canine manner, for I knew only too well that she, with her limited

The three of us adjust to life without Popsie Miranda.

language skills, would not be able to follow my line of reasoning.

Gradually, life returned to normal, or as normal as life could be without Popsie Miranda. Although I too would have preferred to have my darling daughter with us, since I could not, I made the adjustment with the acceptance so characteristic of canines.

Lo and behold. One day I woke up and realized that normality had become a life without Popsie Miranda. Time had worked its curative powers and I only hoped, for Ma's sake, that it hastened to do the same for her.

As we all settled into this new way of life, contentment once more reigned supreme. My health remained good. The *boys* were growing up nicely. The remaining *girls* were as much a joy as they had always been. And Ma was still Ma. She used to say, only half-joking, "I am the Tum Tum Mother. Very privileged to be the Mother of Her Galactic Majesty, Tum Tum, Centre of the Universe." She firmly believed that I had such a potent personality that on some level I must consider myself to be the centre of the universe.

To an extent, Ma was right. Each of us is the centre of our own universe, though of course our external universe is also central to us. It is the relationship one has with the two that is the key to a good and happy life.

I recognized that I was luckier than most. Being a Springer

Spaniel, I had been born with a natural predisposition to both goodness and happiness. Had I been unlucky, I might have been born another breed of dog, maybe even another species of animal. Then I would have had more challenges in life aside from the only major one I actually did, which was having to cope with the mild disability that the car accident caused with my hind quarters. But I was lucky. Not only was I created for love and happiness by virtue of my breed, but I had always had good health, good looks, good care and a good family life.

What really lifted my destiny beyond that of most Springer Spaniels, however, was being Ma's first-born. She firmly believed in self-actualization. As far as she was concerned, I was a sentient being who had potential. Her role, as she saw it, was to develop it. This she set about doing from the day she got me. Showering me with love, which she always tempered with life-enhancing discipline, she encouraged me to express myself. And express myself I did. As eloquently as I could.

Ma never disparaged my attempts at conversation with her. She always talked to me as if I were an intelligent being capable of understanding. She listened when I replied, and tried to make sense of what I was saying; converting my barks and yaps into English and repeating them back to me for verification. Every now and then , she got things wrong – sometimes, as with Shadow and Minette, Citoyenne de France, spectacularly so – but by and large we communicated well, with the result that I had grown up enjoying and appreciating the give and take of good conversation.

As all conversationalists know, clear articulation is fundamental to the art. There is little point in embarking upon an exchange of views if one cannot be heard by the recipient of one's thoughts, so I developed a good, clear, strong voice. Ma's dog-loving neighbour Vickie used to laugh and say that "someone ought to bottle that voice and sell it" while her other friends all declared that I was a "real character". Some even said, "Tum Tum is almost human," which they thought was a compliment though I had my reservations when I contrasted the behaviour of certain humans with us canines.

As I settled into old age, conversation became more and more important. Not being able to move around meant that many of my canine pleasures, such as sniffing out things, were curtailed. I would really have been in big trouble if my voice had weakened as well, but fortunately, it was the one thing that remained as strong as ever. Indeed, I had the vocal chords of a dog seven years my junior: strong, rounded, sharp, instead of the thin, hoarse and reedy sound that older dogs often have.

Only too soon, the year had flown by and Christmas was approaching. I always loved Christmas because Ma always made so much of it. There would be the inevitable fir tree grazing the ceiling in the drawing room at Haresfield, whose ceilings were over fourteen feet high. There would be the usual plethora of presents radiating out from under the tree, thirty or forty for each of the *boys* as well as a quantity of large and small stockings crammed to capacity for us *girls*. As soon as Ma opened the drawing room door, the *boys* and I would rush in followed by the other *girls*. Santa would have placed the presents in neat piles for each person. Ma would direct me to mine, into which I would bury my snout as I sought to consume something right then and there. Ma would always ration out the variety of doggie chocolates, bones, and chewy toys, chew sticks, canine sweets, and squeaky toys over the following weeks, which to me meant that Christmas came not once a year, but every day for the weeks following Christmas Day.

Christmas morning 2000 was much like all our other Haresfield Christmases, except that Popsie Miranda was no longer with us. Although I had made the adjustment to her absence in true canine fashion, Ma, being human, had not, and, as she fed me a particularly succulent beef chew, she told me how odd it seemed to be celebrating without Popsie Miranda.

Although neither she nor I knew it yet, this would also be my last Christmas on earth. I am therefore glad that I enjoyed it as much as I did. I even managed on several occasions to scoff some of the *boys'* Christmas pudding, which they quietly placed on the ground for me when they had eaten their share. (They were good brothers. They were always steering food my way.) I loved Christmas pudding, especially when it was swimming in the brandy butter which Ma always made herself. Fortunately, my stomach was like a steel trap, so there were no unfortunate consequences, though that New Year's Eve some friends of

Ma fed me so much of their leftovers that I nearly had an accident when Ma was taking me out for my final pit stop. She barely had time to hitch up my rigging before a flood reminiscent of Niagara Falls combining with a cannon ball run came pouring out of me to the accompaniment of a chorus of flatuses.

Enjoying my last Christmas at Haresfield.

I used to love taking the air in the doorway at Bourne Street.

That one moment aside, I remained a veritable picture of regularity and stalwart if ancient good health. Although in the aftermath of Popsie Miranda's death Ma had said that she needed to prepare herself for my eventual demise, my continuing strength and vigour seemed to have shoved that idea to the back of her mind. Indeed, she had recently started to say, "It looks as if you're going to be around for a very long time, Tum Tum."

I sincerely hoped so. I loved my life. All sorts of new and exciting things were happening, not the least of which was that the *boys* were devising new games to play with us as they grew up And Ma had started writing a new book. This was always a pleasure for her canine children, for she would sit at her desk for hours on end, breaking off from time to time to give us treats or to take us for quick walks. Or just to stroke us or talk to us, while we joyfully received her attention and otherwise basked in her loving presence.

At Haresfield enjoying the garden during what Ma knew would be my last time.

Wednesday, 28th March, 2001 dawned like any other day. After our usual session in the park, I had my breakfast and settled down to a mid-morning snooze while Ma dressed for a lunch date she was having with a friend who was helping her with background information for her new book. She woke me up when she was ready to leave, taking me out into the back garden with Maisie Carlotta and Maud for a quick pit stop. I confess I was surprised to have fallen into such a deep sleep, but I wasn't exactly discomfited. After all,

I was over 110 in the canine equivalent of 15 human years and 8 months. I would have been unreasonable indeed to expect my energy levels to remain as high as they had once been, so when Ma settled me back onto the sofa and whizzed a quick kiss across my forehead prior to shooting out the front door, I lay down contentedly with Maisie Carlotta snuggling beside me and Maud beside her.

By pure chance, Ma returned home early. "You will never believe it," she said to us, knowing very well that we would understand every word. "Christina got a telephone call in the middle of lunch from her daughter's bank manager to say that someone has stolen Annabel's identity and was in the bank right then trying to draw out a large sum of money. Because Annabel is a minor, Christina had to hightail it to the bank while the manager detained the thief under some pretext or the other. Never a dull moment, eh?"

Normally, Ma would have gone straight from lunch to pick the *boys* up from school, but with an hour to spare, she came back instead to be with us. This was just as well, for had she not settled down to reading a book beside me, she would never have witnessed what happened next. She was idly stroking me when I stiffened. Although I have no recollection of what happened afterwards, Ma not only told enough people in my presence for me to know, but also, now that I am in Pet Heaven and can see all that happened to me during my lifetime, I can provide an actual eye-witness account.

Ma put down the book, looked and saw that my eyes were glazed over and I was shaking and stiff, and immediately started to say, "Oh my God, Tum Tum, you can't be dying." As I continued to throb stiffly, she was convinced I was having a heart attack, so she started to tell me good-bye while stroking me gently. But when the attack continued long past when I should have been dead, she realized that something else was happening, so, running to get her mobile telephone which was sitting on her desk at the opposite end of the double reception room, she called our London vets as she ran back to me. One of the nurses who knew and loved me answered the phone and said it sounded as if I was having a fit. "They're always more distressing to witness than to experience," she said. "She won't be in pain and she won't be conscious while it's going on, so wait until the attack has passed, then bring her in," she said.

By this time, the attack was tapering off, so Ma waited a few minutes until I was resting peacefully before lifting me into her arms and taking me to the car, which was fortunately parked opposite our house.

The vet needed to examine me only cursorily before he said that the nurse's diagnosis of a fit sounded right. Kidney failure, it turned out, was one of the commonest causes of death in older dogs. To make sure that his suspicion of the condition was accurate, he took blood, some of which he looked at then and there. He told Ma he was sending the remainder away to the lab for verification. But he was almost positive that kidney failure was the problem. Fits are the classic symptom.

"Can you operate?" my indomitable Ma, who never gave up without doing her utmost to solve any problem, wanted to know.

"I'm afraid not."

"What about dialysis?"

"That's not an option," he said, then looked at my notes. "I see she's nearly sixteen years old. She's had a good innings. I think the time has come."

This was the second time in almost a year Ma had heard the words she dreaded more than any others. "Time has come for what?" she said, not sure whether he was saying I was dying or should be put down.

"You should consider putting her to sleep," he said.

After Ma had refused that option, she asked what would happen if nature were allowed to take its course. "Once the kidneys fail, the toxins build up in the body. She'll have more and more fits until finally her organs will shut down and she will die."

"Will it be painful?" Ma asked as she stroked me. Her emanations of grief were so powerful that I started to yap consolingly, covering her hand with kisses. She bent down to kiss me as her tears splashed onto my head.

"No. It's going to be worse for you than for her," he said, repeating what the nurse had said. "Watching her fitting might do your head in. I'll prescribe muscle relaxants for you to crush up and feed to her when the time comes. That will relieve the worst of the symptoms. In the meantime, give her these tablets which will assist the kidneys and don't worry if she drinks a lot of water."

"You're sure she's not going to be in pain?" Ma asked anxiously.

"I'm sure," he said.

"How long are we looking at?"

"That depends on so many variables I wouldn't want to hazard a guess. But I don't think we're speaking about months, or even weeks."

The thing with having a robust constitution is that you fight off death the way you fought off disease. Although I wasn't well and certainly didn't feel my customarily vibrant self, I was still Tum Tum. True, I was drinking much more than usual and relieving myself much less. But I was still eating. And I didn't have another fit for the rest of that whole week. Had it not been for the amount of water I was consuming, Ma might have been able to convince herself that I was going to be all right. But, because of it, she knew the problem persisted, and decided to take me that weekend to see John, our country vet, for a second opinion. Regrettably, he could hold out no more hope than our London vets did. Like them, he too was thinking in terms of days, maybe a week if we were incredibly lucky, but no more.

When you're dying, there can be joy intermingled with the sadness. That Saturday evening, our neighbours Vickie and Anna and their son Oliver, that beautiful Welsh Springer Spaniel who was the biggest wuss you could ever hope to meet and who was always hiding behind Vickie's skirts, came over for dinner. A usual, he took one look at all of us and fled behind Vickie. I started to tell him that he'd better come and say goodbye while the going was good. Vickie said, laughingly, "I have to capture that bark for posterity." She promptly ran back to her house in the old stable block a hundred or so yards from us, to fetch her video camera. She returned brandishing it triumphantly. "Come on Tum Tum," she said, "Give us one of those famous barks."

If she thought I would not do so, or didn't understand, she was sorely mistaken. I barked and barked to my heart's content, telling her how much I enjoyed our friendship, even Oliver's wussiness, and how I would keep a nice spot warm for her and Oliver whenever I finally went to Pet Heaven, so that they would not feel lonely when they too arrived there. Although Vickie did not understand all that I was saying, she was certainly enjoying our communication, and told Ma that she would have a cassette made so that Ma would always have a record of my inimitable bark.

Ma, meanwhile, was laughing. "I swear, Tum Tum is the biggest ham since Laurence Olivier. Neither age nor illness can dim that voice. Just listen to how young and carefree and happy she sounds," Ma said, mimicking my bark.

This was a genuinely happy moment for all of us. Rather less joyful were Vickie and Anna's tears the following afternoon when they came by to tell me goodbye. Even Oliver greeted me with a friendly sniff instead of bolting behind Vickie the way he usually did, which told me that he was picking up the scent of decline. We dogs often do that.

I returned to London that Sunday evening. I was fine on Monday and Tuesday. But on Wednesday night I had another fit right after we had done a quick tour of the back garden preparatory to going upstairs to bed. I could tell from Ma's pores that she was filled with dread; a feeling confirmed when she telephoned the veterinary clinic to provide the update the vet had told her she should. "Bring her in," an Australian locum suggested, so Ma bundled me into the car and drove us there.

For the first time since I was a puppy, neither Ma nor I knew anyone at the clinic. All the usual nurses were off duty. So too were the vets. And it was our bad luck that we ended up with a medico who was aggressively in favour of euthanasia and had no respect for anyone who didn't agree with her.

The trouble started as soon as this woman had had a look at me. "I'll prepare the solution," she declared in a matter of fact tone of voice, her pores oozing the fragrance of anticipation that the power to take life clearly held for her – or maybe it was the fat fee she would be earning for an out-of-hours termination. She wheeled around and headed with decided jauntiness to the medicine cabinet across the room.

"What solution are you talking about?" Ma said.

"To put her to sleep," she said to Ma as if she were a genius and Ma a fool.

I could hardly believe this woman's insensitivity. But I need not have feared. Ma had never been a pushover and she definitely wasn't about to start now.

"If you look at the notes, you will see that I don't want euthanasia but that you will provide muscle relaxants when the time comes, which I presume means now," she said sharply.

"I can't believe you plan to waltz out of here with a dying dog, instead of having her put to sleep peacefully," this obnoxious woman said authoritatively.

"I didn't come here for moral instruction from someone who patently doesn't have a frame of reference for it," Ma said in her iciest tone. "Please give me the medication your colleagues agreed to provide last week, so that we can bring this most disagreeable encounter to a close."

Crossing to the medication cupboard, the woman popped something into an envelope. "You can have one tablet. If you want any more, you'll have to come back tomorrow. I'll be issuing instructions that you are to be given only one at a time," she spat before shooting next door to the nurses' desk to prepare the bill.

When she had done so, rather than bringing it back in to us, which anyone with any consideration would have done considering that I couldn't walk, she called to Ma to come and collect it. "I'll be right back," Ma said to me gently, leaving me on the examining table. She stepped into the doorway linking the two rooms, and, extending her hand for the bill, said, "If you want me to see that, you will have to bring it to me," thereby forcing this ghastly woman to step away from the desk and hand it to her.

Ma looked down, saw that she was being charged £5 for one Valium tablet, and her eyebrows shot up so much I thought they were going to hit the ceiling. "If this is your attempt to punish me for failing to give you a fat fee for killing my dog, or a ploy to milk my dog's condition for your financial benefit, you will discover that you bear more than a passing resemblance to Pyrrhus," Ma said as the room exploded with the scent of rage.

Ma stepped out of view, plainly with the intention of putting the bill on the desk, and I overheard her saying, "I have never in my life met a more disagreeable woman than you, and I've come across some pretty dreadful corkers in my time."

Just then, Ma stepped back into the examining room as she was saying, "I require this invoice to be submitted to me through the post." She was shaking with anger to such an extent that I had to yap out a consoling message to her as she was lifting me.

Once I was in Ma's arms, I licked her cheek, which was something I seldom did, for she ordinarily didn't like dogs licking faces, but in the circumstances it seemed appropriate. Understanding perfectly, she nuzzled me and said, "Don't you worry, Tum Tum. As long as you draw breath, it's my joy and privilege to take the best care of you I can come up with. Now let's get out of here before I say or do something I regret."

We had now reached the front door, which was obviously shut, this being a veterinary clinic in central London. The vet, who was so eager to waft me into Paradise before Ma, Nature or I were ready for the transition, stood, hands folded defiantly across her meagre chest. She glared at us as if to say, "Since you're both so able, open the door yourself." But Ma was having none of her nonsense. "In all the years I have been coming here, I have never seen anyone expect someone with a dog in her arms to open a door for themselves. Unless you begin conducting yourself up to the standard I have always been used to here, you can rest assured I will telephone Keith Butt (who owned the practice) and tell him I will not be budging from this spot until this door is opened for me. Whether by you, by him, or by someone else is of no consequence to me. There are only two certainties in life at the moment. The first is that you will not be killing my dog and being rewarded for doing so, and the second is that my fingers will not be touching that door handle tonight."

Deciding that I had better add my voice to Ma's, I barked that I wanted to get home as soon as possible, so she'd better open the door for us. Whether it was me or Ma who convinced her that it would be wiser to co-operate than obstruct, I do not know, but she crossed the room, opened the door, and, no sooner were we out of it, than she slammed it so forcefully that I swear the building vibrated.

"Unbelievable," Ma said.

"Absolutely," I yapped in return. "But thanks for being such a protective Ma. I certainly wouldn't have wanted that woman to be the architect of my transition. Not when we haven't even prepared the *girls* and the *boys* for my departure."

As anyone can appreciate, after such an unpleasant experience, neither Ma nor I wanted to go back to the clinic lest we should run

Ma took this one of me on the Thursday morning.

As you can see, on Thursday evening I was still in pretty good shape.

across this ghastly woman again. So the following morning Ma telephoned John in the country and asked him if she could give me Xanax, which she had in the house, instead of Valium. He said yes. He suggested that she crush it up and mix it in my food. It would help to relax me and lower the intensity of the fits, which from hereon in would increase in frequency. "And when she goes off her food, which she will soon do as the toxins build up more and more in her body, put the powder from the crushed tablets in the flap on the side of her mouth between her teeth and her lips. That way her body will absorb it."

Humour is never far from the surface on even the saddest of occasions, and so it proved on this occasion. By that afternoon, Ma realized that she would have to get a prescription for more Xanax from her doctor, so she rang up his office, only to learn that he was away on holiday. One of his colleagues was covering for him, so the nurse, who knew Ma well, asked him for a prescription. She thought better of informing him that it was for a dog, and he wrote out the standard number of tablets. On Friday morning, Ma realized that she would run short over the weekend if she did not get another prescription filled, so she telephoned Liz again. "Are you sure this lady doesn't have a problem with this drug?" he queried, astonished that anyone would need more tablets so quickly. "Actually, she does have a problem, it just not what you think it is," Liz confessed. "Her dog's dying of kidney failure and the vet tried to stick her for five quid per tablet." "Then she must have as many tablets as she needs," he said, and promptly wrote out a prescription that was so generous that Ma still has some of the tablets nearly a decade after my death.

By Friday afternoon, it was obvious that I was fading fast. I, who Ma used to say was aptly named because I loved my food so much, was now off it altogether. That was an unmistakable sign, not only to me, but to Ma and the *girls*. How sweet they were. They came up to me, giving me all the sniffs, licks, body grazes and kisses any grandmother and great-grandmother would want. Because we canines have a protocol whereby we retire to die, they would then leave me in peace just in case I wanted that, though they always returned periodically to check on whether I wanted some love or to be left alone.

If the *girls* displayed canine etiquette, Ma was a veritable paradigm of human attentiveness. The only time she left me alone was when she took Maisie Carlotta and Maud to the park for their runs. Otherwise, she remained solidly and quietly by my side.

I was still conscious, though the fits were coming more and more frequently. Although I was never conscious during them, I cannot say I felt great when I was conscious, but then, I wasn't in pain either, and as my life was ebbing away, I was glad that it was doing so at home, surrounded by my loved ones. I was also glad that Ma had decided not to take us to the country that weekend. The two hour drive would have been too much.

By Saturday morning, I had weakened so much that Ma did not expect me to last the day. She called the *boys* into our bedroom and told them that they must say goodbye the way they had done with Popsie Miranda. Being a year older and wiser, they appreciated more so than they had with my late daughter that we were about to embark upon a relatively long separation. So they hugged and stroked and kissed me, telling me how much they loved me. "You mustn't forget to thank her for all the joy she brought into your lives," Ma said, to which Dmitri replied, "Thanks for being such a good horsey when we were young, Tum Tum." Both boys started to giggle as they remembered those happy times, and Michael added, "Thanks for saving my life on the toboggan." Summoning up whatever strength I still had, I yapped my appreciation, licked them, then had to lay my head back down as weakness overcame me once more.

I did not die that day, though I did become semi-comatose that evening.

Sunday, 8th April 2001 was one of those grey, chilly overcast days that are so characteristic of London. It matched Ma's frame of mind as I slid into a deeper and deeper coma. Even though at that stage I was oblivious to everything, Ma kept on grinding up the muscle relaxants and placing the powder in the folds of my mouth to lessen the intensity of the fits, which were now recurring with, for her, frightening frequency. The vets and nurse had been right. Watching me depart this way was far harder on her than it was on me. But she did not shirk what

Ma put me on our bed and stroked me until I had crossed over into Pet Heaven.

she regarded as her duty and privilege. As far as she was concerned, this process was also a way of honouring me and the relationship we had had. So she sat on her bed reading and stroking me while I lay on the floor beside her on vet-bed padded out with newspaper.

Fearing that she might miss the moment when it came, Ma had the *boys'* bring her supper up to her in the bedroom. Afterwards, she moved me onto the bed while she watched television with the *boys* and the other *girls*. She sat there stroking, stroking, and stroking me, aware that only too soon there would be no further opportunity to do so. She was running her left hand over my side at 10:37 when I gasped, took my last breath, and was gone.

It had been a good life and indeed I had had a good innings, being four months short of the venerable (for a Springer Spaniel) age of sixteen human years. My only hope was that Ma wouldn't grieve too much.

Chapter Thirteen

I had always been adventurous, which is how I came to be run over by that car when I was nine months old. Nothing, however, prepared me for the adventure that crossing over from earth to Pet Heaven was.

As I drew my last breath, I became aware of being surrounded by the most brilliant white light. Despite its brightness, there was no element of discomfort the way there had been on earth when you looked up at the sun too suddenly. What struck me was the extraordinary clarity and lightness of feeling which accompanied this light.

As I looked, fascinated, I saw that I was in the most beautiful place imaginable. It was immediately obvious that Pet Heaven had much in common with earth, in that there were beautiful fields, magnificent mountains, delightful streams, though the scale and scope put poor little earth to shame. I detected beaches to my left and snow-capped peaks to my right in the distance. Here, I could tell immediately, was a place where everything was good and bountiful without end.

Just as I was taking in all the physical wonders, Popsie Miranda and Sootie bowled up to me, tails wagging in greeting. Before they even had a chance to bark out a welcome, I knew that they were there to welcome me to my new home.

Our loved ones, I was about to learn, are even more important to us in Pet Heaven than they were on earth. And, humans will be pleased to learn, harmony reigns in a way it has never done on earth, so all the petty squabbles and divisions that separate beings on earth no longer exist.

Although Popsie Miranda and Sootie were instantly recognizable, they had definitely changed since leaving earth. While they were now older than they had been when I had last seen them, neither of them had degenerated with age the way we all did on earth. Without becoming younger, they had become better, more beautiful versions of themselves. They also had magnificent tails topped with the most stunning white fur. This was a surprise, for both their tails had been docked when they were five day old puppies, yet here they were, wagging these splendiferous communicants of pleasure.

Before I had a chance to wonder whether my tail would grow back as well, they were upon me, sniffing and licking and yapping affectionately. It was then that I realized that I was walking. More than that, I was walking perfectly. For the first time since my accident when I was nine months old, I had the mobility I was born to possess. Overjoyed at the restoration of my powers, I gambolled with them as they took me on a quick introductory tour. "Pet Heaven is a world without end. Literally without end," Popsie Miranda explained. "It is infinite. No matter how far you go, or for how long, you will never come to the end of it, because it has no end. Everyone and everything that has ever lived are here. It's so immense that it takes everyone awhile to get their heads around that fact."

"What a shock Ma will have when she comes up here. She won't be able to call me the centre of the universe anymore," I quipped.

"You'll love it here. Everyone does. Come, we have all sorts of loved ones waiting to meet you," Sootie said.

With that, I ran after them as they headed towards a Palladian style villa set in its own park which belonged to Sootie's earthly grandmother, who was housing us until Pa and Ma leave earth. There, I met a variety of ancestors and relations: brothers, sisters, parents, grand-parents, even cousins and friends, all of whom were living happily with or nearby this dog-loving human. I was delighted to see Charley and Popsie's other puppy who had died of a cleft palate, as well as Il Magnifico and John's Bella, all of whom were now fully grown and in splendid health. "There are so many dogs for you to meet that you won't have a moment to yourself for the foreseeable future," Popsie Miranda said.

Just then Ma's brother Uncle Mickey dropped in. He had heard that I had arrived and, knowing that Ma would want him to greet me, had come to do so. He had not been a dog-lover on earth, so I was surprised to see him. But when I remembered how kind he had always been, I understood what had prompted him to come. We had a good laugh about the picture I had chewed up, and he said, "It's never going to be framed, you know. Your Ma has it rolled up and it will remain rolled up until she comes here, at which time it's going to be thrown out. No one is going to realize it's a valuable painting, albeit less valuable than it would have been without your contribution."

"I am really sorry I chewed it up," I said.

"You don't need to have any regrets on my account," Uncle Mickey said. "I was to blame, not you. I am the one who locked you out of the drawing room and stupidly left the bedroom door open."

"Does everyone resolve their differences in Pet Heaven as readily as you and I are doing?" I asked Uncle Mickey.

"Some do so more quickly than others," he replied, and I realized that in this marvellous place everyone understood everyone else's language. "But ultimately, the positive resolution of differences is one of the functions of Heaven. You see, there's no difference between Pet Heaven and Human Heaven. We are all here to live good, happy, harmonious lives. You'll be surprised to see how many different roads there are to happiness. Tomorrow, I'll take you to the Ghetto where you can see some of earth's wickedest people voluntarily making amends to those they injured. Pol Pot, the Cambodian dictator, for instance, has set himself the task of cleaning out the lavatory of each and every person he harmed. He'll be deep in the muck for many a millennium to come. I'll take you to see him in action. He welcomes onlookers. It's a way of humbling himself and expatiating his crimes."

What's a dog to say to such an extraordinary state of affairs? Of course I knew who Pol Pot was. I used to hear about his atrocities on the television evening news. So I nodded sagely, which Uncle Mickey took as the cue to continue. "Afterwards, we can go to the premiere of the latest piano concerto Beethoven has composed for Liszt. I know how much you loved Ludwig's four piano concerti and Franz's B Minor Sonata when we were on earth. I remember how you used to place your head in your Ma's lap and listen with eyes closed and tail gently wagging in time to the music. The concert is being held in the Michael Jackson Auditorium for Classical and Popular Music. And don't think you'll be the only pet in attendance. Here all music-loving animals are encouraged to attend concerts with or without humans."

"Are they well attended?" I asked, wondering whether I would see a few or a lot of other dogs. "You'll be gobsmacked at the immensity of the venue and the variety of animals who are there. I bet it never occurred to you that hippopotamuses are really into classical music? And I know you've won't have seen the amazing aerial musical shows that Bugsby Berkeley has been choreographing for butterflies ever since he left earth. No one on earth had any idea that butterflies are not only terribly musical, but also excellent at aerial dances. Believe me, Tum Tum, you will love them. Especially as how he's recently entered into a musical partnership with Fritz Lowe and Alan Jay Lerner, so everyone is eagerly anticipating their new show."

What could a dog say to all this? "Fascinating," was all I could come up with.

Like all music lovers, Uncle Mickey needed no further encouragement to share the musical delights he could introduce me to. Without even pausing to draw breath, he continued, "And the acoustics for all these recitals are incredible. Far better than anything worldly. Here we have the finest experts from all the ancient and contemporary earthly civilizations, and they've been running apprenticeship programmes for centuries for people who didn't know they had a particular talent until they were exposed to that knowledge here in Heaven. The result is that technical expertise has been raised to a fine art here."

Uncle Mickey bent down, stroked me, and said, "I've got to get back to work, so come give me a goodbye kiss on the cheek."

I was astonished. Not only had he not been a dog lover, but he knew that Ma didn't allow us to kiss humans on their faces. Seeing my expression, he reassured me, "Here you can kiss anyone without fear of infection. So forget what your Ma told you about not licking humans. You can even lick us on the lips if you please, though I personally prefer cheek licks to lip licks."

Before Uncle Mickey's figure had retreated into the near distance, I said to Popsie Miranda, "Work. Did Uncle Mickey say he's going back to work? Do people work in Heaven?

"Not only people," Popsie Miranda yapped. "Everyone works in Heaven. Whether human or animal or even fish, everyone has an occupation and makes a contribution to life. The fish tend the oceans, keeping them in good working order. They scour the sea beds and look after coral reefs. They also look after each other and entertain themselves when they're not working. Everyone else does the equivalent. You won't believe the functions various animals have up here. Talents that weren't apparent on earth proliferate here. There's no idleness in Heaven, not that that means there isn't relaxation and rest, for there is. But everyone and everything is in accord with the true purposes of life, which are fulfilment, contentment, harmony, constructiveness, and gainful occupation."

In the days to come, I began to appreciate what an amazing place Heaven is. All living things, fish as well as animals (humans included) and even plants, had crossed over to the eternal world, and were obliged to live eternally in harmony. There was a spirit of co-operation that you never found on earth. No one was ever bored or lonely. A lifetime of perpetual interest, harmony, and accomplishment awaited everyone. Because all living things could not die again, gone were the days when lions feasted on wildebeest, sharks gobbled up sea lions, and humans ate whatever other living being they fancied. This meant that the food industry in Heaven was even bigger business than it had been on earth, for of course everyone, man as well as beast, had to be fed. It was incredible to behold how inventive everyone in the food industry was, for while meat-eating was no longer possible, all carnivores still liked the taste of meat. So alternatives had had to be created.

And what alternatives they turned out to be. Substitutes for meat had been devised chemically by scientists. These looked, smelt and tasted exactly like the originals. If you wanted rare 'steak', it oozed 'blood' as convincingly as if you had been to the abattoir and carted off a choice slice of heifer. 'Duck' was something of a favourite in certain quarters when I first crossed over, though I would discover soon enough that 'pheasant' cooked in red onions and red wine a la *Gaillac* became all the rage for about three weeks shortly afterwards, before 'partridge' stuffed with dates and cooked in pastry replaced it for a longer run.

Fashion, I was surprised to see, was every bit as prevalent in Heaven as it had been on earth. Everything, from food and clothes to transport vehicles and entertainment, whether in the form of films, television, live concerts, or jamborees, was as subject to the whims of fashion as they had been on earth. In fact, time would show me it was even more so, largely, I suspect, because things would be very dull indeed if novelty were not an intrinsic element in the kaleidoscope that is life, and Heavenly life is both longer and more varied than earthly life ever was. By giving us all a great deal of scope for keeping ourselves occupied as well as entertained, fashion is even more prevalent in Heaven than it was on earth.

As you can imagine, with fashion being a constant eternally, there is a whole industry dedicated not only to it but to the promulgation of news about what is in and what is out. The editors of newspapers and magazines are every bit as influential here as Anna Wintour was on earth. And there are so many 'television' programmes on the latest trends that all the Parisians trendsetters from the eighteenth century to the twenty first centuries like Rose Bertin, Worth, Balenciaga, St Laurent, and McQueen will forever exult in the resurgence of a gift they had thought long lost, but which has seen their stardom perpetuated eternally.

And this being Heaven, where everyone is generous and shares a gift rather than jealously clinging to it, these trendsetters have trained up a whole new batch of superstars, who will in turn train up others, for today's train driver might move on in a decade or a century or a millennium or two to develop an interest in clothing and become yet another fashion icon. The beauty of infinity is that with an infinite amount of time and an infinite amount of co-operation and encouragement people have infinite opportunities for the development of skills, talents and interests they did not even know they possessed. Though it has to be said that even in Heaven each of us has natural endowments, and it was a lot easier for Uncle Mickey, who on earth had always wanted to become a musician instead of the lawyer his parents made him become, to become the accomplished pianist he now is, than for Ma. She just doesn't have the aptitude, though in three or four thousand years she will achieve the level of accomplishment that Uncle Mickey had after a few months.

As you can imagine, if fashion in all its forms is big business, so are manufacturing and shopping. This, I know, will come as welcome news to many a businessman and shopaholic. The beauty of those Heavenly industries is that there is no exploitation the way there was on earth. Because greed no longer exists and fairness is a guiding principle for all, there are no more sweat shops turning out attractive but cheap clothing. The finest silks and furs are made from chemical compounds and produced in attractive factories where people who enjoy sewing, pattern-making, fabric-cutting and all the other attendant processes for the manufacturing of garments, produce them for a fair wage. No one in Heaven is poor. Of course, some people are still richer than others, but since enviousness no longer exists, those who wish to work less do not mind if those who work more make more money (yes, money still exists – but it is no longer the bone of contention it used to be on earth. It is now a straightforward means of exchange with its value willingly acknowledged by all). And since the rich do not consider themselves to be any better than their poorer brethren – snobbishness having also gone the way of envy and greed – there is welcome harmony in the multiplicity of a richly textured society.

Of course, we doggies were never envious on earth, so we never had any of those conflicts which so bedevilled humans. But greed was another matter altogether. I could hardly believe how I reacted when I had my first dinner in Pet Heaven. It was so unlike the way I had been on earth that I was almost tempted to ask Popsie Miranda to introduce me to this new Tum Tum. For, having eaten a nice bowl of 'chicken' and rice mixed with the most delicious vegetables, I stopped voluntarily when my stomach said it had had enough.

Could this be me? Tum Tum. Who loved her food so much she could eat endlessly. Who had been so aptly named, as Ma used to say. I confess to being taken unawares. Indeed, I was so surprised I looked around wondering if the answer existed outside of myself. Which, it emerged, it did.

Popsie Miranda laughed and said, "In Heaven no one eats more than they need to. Because there is always enough for everyone, we do not need to stock up on extra supplies the way we were instinctively impelled to do on earth. You'll notice when you've been here for awhile that no one is too fat or too thin. That's another manifestation of the balance that comes with being in harmony with your nature and your surroundings."

I must confess, I was not quite sure about this latest development. I had been an ardent student of the Gordon Gekko school of greed-being-good. But no resistance to this unwelcome turn of events welled up within me. Instead, my greed sloughed off so effortlessly and was replaced so definitely by the serene acceptance of this new way of being that I barely had time to yap out my consent before I turned tail and left my great-grandmother's full bowl of 'quail' and pasta mixed with broccoli with all the alacrity of a well-fed Springer Spaniel who had successfully surrendered to a new and better way of living.

This new place, I quickly came to see, was fascinating beyond comparison. In some ways, it was so similar to earth, yet in other ways so radically different, that one was transfixed. Take, for instance, the question of food. Although all meat and many other things like bread, sweets, snacks, cakes and confectionary (even canine confectionary) were chemically engineered and then manufactured, plants still grew in Heaven (everyone needs their fruit and vegetables if they are going to have a balanced diet) and plant produce was harvested in much the same way as it had been on earth. This meant that some farms opted for the age-old way of growing and reaping by hand, while the more efficient super-farms grew and harvested their crops with super-efficient means of production and mechanized harvesting the like of which was unimaginable on earth when I was there.

If anything, getting fruit and vegetables from the farms to the supermarkets in Heaven was as challenging as it had been on earth. The logistics remained intricate, in that there were still vast distances to be covered between the field where the crop grew and the place where it was sold. There were still vast transports to be loaded, with both humans and animals involved in the task.

The one thing that Heaven has over earth is that the produce doesn't decay. Not, I have to tell you, that it hangs about for long. With all those mouths to feed, everything is consumed pretty smartly, and the other thing that makes Heaven so different from earth is that there is no wastage. Living as we do in a conscionable, thoughtful, considerate environment, where no one takes more than they need and no one wants to disrespect themselves or the greater good by exceeding their needs, there is neither wilful waste nor woeful want.

Although humans are invariably struck by the many similarities between their earthly and heavenly existences when they first arrive here, they are always surprised by the role we animals occupy up here. We enjoy a degree of respect and independence we seldom possessed on earth, our roles as intelligent, sentient beings finally acknowledged even by those religious souls who used to preach that we were soulless.

I am sure that one of the things that has made it easy for homo *sapiens* to see the error of their ways is that their powers of comprehension have expanded now that they are freed from the chains of gravity. Because they can finally understand what we are saying, they can no longer delude themselves into thinking that we are 'dumb'. This has been a welcome change, I can tell you.

It is always amusing to see the extent to which many of them are shocked by our wisdom and intelligence. And make no mistake about it; we cultivate our minds now that we have the opportunity. Education is as important to many of us as it is to any human scholar. We go to school and to university whenever we wish to learn new skills, just like our human brethren. Indeed, at the moment, I am doing my Doctorate in Communication, which will come as no surprise to Ma when she hears about it, for she always said that I was a born communicator, and it turns out she was right.

I am also the president of my university's debating society, and have recently introduced multi-species debates. Our secretary is a former dog-catcher from 16th century York in the north of England, who makes amends for his earthly cruelty to us by taking the minutes of our monthly committee meetings. He reads these back to us every month, the look on his face being a study in bemused enlightenment which never fails to elicit one of Popsie Miranda's unmistakable smiles.

In fact, he's become a great friend of mine, and often accompanies me for the swims I take every few days in the lake near our house. He finds my 'take' on life so intriguing that I invariably have to remind him that it is bad practice to swim and talk, unless you want to swallow water. "You're just so interesting," he says. "I always want to find out what you're thinking." So we discourse on whatever the topic of the day is. Or, to be more accurate, I let him talk while I swim, taking care to keep my head well above water and my mouth tightly shut. Which isn't always easy, I can tell you, for his enthusiasm so often gets the better of him that he coughs and splutters from the water he has gulped, and it takes all my self-restraint to keep from laughing out aloud and swallowing a huge mouthful myself.

When I am not at university, I work in customer relations at the local train and tram station. I love the job, because I have always been friendly, outgoing, and helpful, though I do not envisage staying in it for much longer. I can tell that I am already outgrowing it and will soon need something that offers me more scope.

Although trams and trains are all very well for getting around, individuals who like challenges, as I do, need something more exciting. Not that the tram and train service don't offer scope for those who like placid lives. The scale of the service is beyond anything people on earth could ever have imagined it would be. The multitude of individuals of various sizes and species that have to be moved from place to place on a daily basis is staggering. This means that we require coaches of a variety of sizes, from relatively small to huge, for remember, we have everything from mice to elephants as well as humans travelling back and forth. After one of the trains lurched some years ago and an elephant called Tobin toppled onto a lion and winded him severely (in Heaven there are no broken bones or serious injuries), the Minister for Transport decided that it made more sense to give everyone the choice between co-existent trains or coaches that are categorized according to size. So now we can take our chances of too adventurous a ride or one that is more sedate and certain. Personally, I prefer the excitement of the mixed carriages.

Aside from trains and trams, we also have ships of various sizes for getting about on the seas, just like on earth, as well as aeroplanes. But planes, such as everyone on earth knows them, are the heavenly version of the bus: People only take them for relatively short hops. Because the distances we have to cover in Pet Heaven can be so much greater than anything an earthling can imagine, we have hyperplanes for longer distances. And for comfort too. These were actually designed many years before I came here by Graf von Zepplin. They are very sophisticated variations of his helium-borne Zepplins which went out of favour after the crash of the Hindenburg in New Jersey before the Second World War. They are the end in convenience as well as sophistication, the contemporary equivalent of Blue Riband ocean liners. They hold as many passengers as ocean liners too, every inch of space being utilized now that Graf von Zepplin has cracked the mystery of fuelling them on enhanced air. Everyone dresses for dinner in formal evening wear, and during the day the beachwear around the swimming pools is enough to keep Elsa Schiaparelli in business for the next millennium at least. I must admit I am looking forward to the day that Ma comes here so that I can treat her to one of these cruises (I am saving up already), for these hyperplanes sweep at almost touching distance over the terrain, some of which is so breathtakingly beautiful that it is no wonder that these cruises have been one of Pet Haven's most popular vacation activities since Zepplin solved the fuel problem in 1962.

I am also hoping to have saved up enough money by then to buy my own airmobile, so that I can zip her around in the heavenly version of the tourer-car. The latest ones are manufactured by Henry Ford, Messrs Daimler and Benz, and the Dodge brothers, who have recently joined force to provide alternatives to the Cadillac/Morris/Ferrari consortium whose vehicles, have been so popular with man and beast for the last fifteen years.

These vehicles are the infinitely more comfortable than aeroplanes. Naturally, they come in a variety of sizes and shapes. Pekingese need smaller airmobiles than springers, whose vehicles are in turn dwarfed by the elephant airmobile. I plan to buy a Packard, because they are they are so practical, being made for a pack of nine spaniels but with enough space to hold two human beings if one wants to cut down the doggie capacity to four.

At the moment, I cannot afford my own airmobile, but it doesn't matter. Popsie Miranda allows me to use hers whenever I want. Her life here has really taken off in ways I could never have foreseen when we were on earth. She has a dual career. On the one hand, she runs a successful perfumery, selling her own brand, *Popsie Miranda's Bouquet des Chiennes Exotiques*, which is presently one of the most popular canine perfumes in the whole of Pet Heaven. She also has a quality control business, which is where her tremendous success started.

When she came up to Pet Heaven, she decided she would put her love of having things in her mouth to good use, and got a job checking that the consistency of the 'pheasant' manufactured by our local eatery was up to its earthly standard by picking each one up and feeling how soft or hard. Although they were usually up to scratch, even in Heaven machines malfunction, so every now and then she would have to bin one rather than put it on the conveyor belt for it to be packaged prior to being sold in the supermarkets.

The owner of the plant, a liver and white Springer Spaniel named Petronius, seems to have been a bit sweet on Popsie Miranda. (Yes, even in Pet Heaven there is romance, though it is without the turgid or jealous overtones of earthly attraction.) As he and Popsie Miranda became closer, he suggested that she become the 'face' of the business. He employed Cecil Beaton and his assistant, my grandson Charley, to photograph her. Before you could say woof, Popsie Miranda's imagine was plastered over packaging all over Pet Heaven. Once that happened, she became so well known that everyone recognized her wherever she went.

Too much attention had never had much appeal for my beloved daughter, so fame did not suit her as much as it would have suited someone of a less retiring disposition. She therefore suggested to Petronius that he get another 'face' and she would work behind the scenes on the quality control aspect alone. This being Pet Heaven, where everyone is fair and greed no longer exists, he not only agreed, but offered her a partnership commensurate with the degree of her input. Which is how she has come to be in charge of one of the most successful spaniel quality control businesses.

One day, while Popsie Miranda was inspecting a batch of 'partridge', a very nice lady came into the factory. She wanted very firm 'partridge' (there is no accounting for strange taste, especially when the person in question is an avid follower of Julia Child and wants to cook game in rich Bordeaux 1957 for four hours), so Popsie Miranda ordered up a special batch for her. While waiting for them to be ready, they got talking. Then the lady said, "You have the most delicious scent. What is it?"

"Oh, just something I brew for myself," Popsie Miranda said.

"Can you replicate it in quantity?"

"I see no reason why not."

"If you'd like to, I'll take as much as you can brew and market it. My business is perfumes. For people, animals, houses, stores, factories, anything that likes scents."

One thing led to another, and just as the perfume was taking off, a reporter with the Heavenly Gazette discovered that Popsie Miranda was the creator. This was news indeed. Everyone remembered that Popsie Miranda had done a Greta Garbo and retired from the public eye at the height of her success. So he asked Popsie if she would mind him letting his readership know. Knowing that today's news wraps tomorrow's fish, she agreed. Just as well too, for this bit of publicity gave the product the boost it needed to ignite, since when *Popsie Miranda's Bouquet des Chiennes Exotiques* has been worn by all sorts of dog-lovers. Even Marie Antoinette was smelt in it last week at a reception Popsie and I attended at the Versailles Costume Ball last week.

You can imagine how proud I am of my daughter's success.

I must admit, I love everything about Pet Heaven. It is truly the most wonderful place. Although no one should be in a rush to get here – that would defeat the very purpose of our earthly existence – once we are here, we can ask for no more than that all our loved ones join us. Which they will, in time.

For my part, I am especially looking forward to seeing Ma and the *boys* again, as well as all the descendants of mine whom Ma keeps on breeding. They may not know me, but I, who can see them, know and love them already. When the time comes, it will be interesting to incorporate the lives we are living now with their lives. And where Ma is concerned, that means each of us adjusting to our heavenly role as both pet and person. I have no doubt she and I and all the rest of us will make the adjustment easily. With love, all things are not only possible but simple. Undeniably, Ma will have to adjust to the fact that I – an all the others - will come and go more freely than we did on earth. I won't be hanging around the house all day the way I used to on earth. Not when I have work to do and a life to lead. But that does not mean that Ma won't be an intrinsic part of my life, for she will be. I will live with her the way I did on earth. All of us will. So, after a day enjoying the benefits and delights that occupation bring in their wake, I will return to Ma's house, where we will all live happily ever after.

..